AUDEN, THE PSALMS, AND ME

AUDEN, THE PSALMS, AND ME

J. CHESTER JOHNSON

Church Publishing
NEW YORK

Church Publishing
19 East 34th Street
New York, NY 10016
www.churchpublishing.org

Cover design by Paul Soupiset
Typeset by Rose Design

Library of Congress Cataloging-in-Publication Data
A record of this book is available from the Library of Congress.

ISBN-13: 978-0-89869-964-7 (pbk.)
ISBN-13: 978-0-89869-965-4 (ebook)

Printed in the United States of America

for Freda, who knew, better than I, the immediate doesn't always displace the important

Contents

Acknowledgments

At the outset, I want to thank David Lehman, the poet, editor, and anthologist, for his curiosity and interest in the retranslation of the psalms by the Episcopal Church, which is the version now included in the Church's Book of Common Prayer, for which W. H. Auden and I crossed paths in the early 1970s, when we served as the two poets on the drafting committee for the retranslation. As a result of David's request that I write about this experience for the Best American Poetry blog, and through the essential assistance of its managing editor, Stacey Harwood, the Best American Poetry blog distributed my initial articles on this subject in 2012: "On Working with W. H. Auden on the Psalms" and "Auden on Prayer Book Revision: No More Mr. Nice Guy?"

I'm also grateful to the editors at the *Papers de Versalia* project in Spain that has issued a series of volumes in Spanish on major poets over the last few years, including Rainer Maria Rilke, Emily Dickinson, Giuseppe Ungaretti, and now, W. H. Auden, the latter volume being entitled *W. H. Auden: Quaderns de Versalia*, in which my own article, "Auden: Defender at Dusk," first appeared in 2014. In turn, I want to thank the staff of the literary journal *Green Mountains Review*, especially its editor-in-chief, Elizabeth Powell, for publishing, also in 2014, the English version of "Auden: Defender at Dusk."

Appreciation is also due to the poet and translator, Ann Cefola, who conducted an extensive interview with me entitled, "After Auden: Retranslating the Psalms." This piece was published in 2015 by the literary journal *Illuminations*; I'm grateful to its editor, Simon Lewis.

Portions of this book build on the contents of the above mentioned and previously published articles, though numerous adjustments have been made to the text of those pieces to incorporate associated concepts, opinions, and historical circumstances into this volume.

I should also extend my thanks to the Archives of the Episcopal Church for giving me the opportunity to examine and use certain archival correspondence from 1967 by W. H. Auden to his parish priest at the time, the Rev. J. C. Michael Allen, and by and between W. H. Auden and the Rev. Canon Charles M. Guilbert from 1967–1968. When this latter correspondence occurred, Canon Guilbert was custodian of the Book of Common Prayer, chairman of the drafting committee for the Episcopal Psalter retranslation project, and an important member of the Standing Liturgical Commission of the Episcopal Church, which functioned as the oversight body for the retranslation and liturgical revisions to the Episcopal Book of Common Prayer. Among other issues, the correspondence between Auden and Guilbert dealt mainly with (1) the retranslation of the Psalter project by the Episcopal Church, then underway; (2) the revision of the entire Book of Common Prayer, also being pursued at that time by the Episcopal Church; and (3) Auden's specific role in and views about various matters related to the Psalter retranslation, including adjustments then being considered for particular psalms, and his individual judgments toward the revision of certain other parts of the Book of Common Prayer. The Archives of the Episcopal Church has also provided to me copies of correspondence between Canon Guilbert and me that I had lost or misplaced over the years, and additionally has conducted several searches through its records to satisfy other ad hoc requests I have made during the writing of this book.

The Rt. Rev. David Stancliffe, who held the position of chairman of the Church of England's Liturgical Commission from 1993 to 2005 when both *Common Worship: Services and Prayers* and *Common Worship: Daily Prayer* were produced and who is acknowledged as a chief architect of the revised version of the psalms embodied in those volumes, was particularly generous in his responses to my inquiries about the various uses of the 1979 Episcopal Psalter both in the development of the *Common Worship* psalms and for worship purposes and services by the Church of England during Dr. Stancliffe's tenure as chairman of the Church of England's Liturgical Commission.

I would definitely be remiss not to express my sincere and deep appreciation to Edward Mendelson, Auden's literary executor and principal biographer. For the last three decades, he has not only been a good friend but also a source of encyclopedic knowledge and enlightened perspective about W. H. Auden; some of my most enjoyable moments have been those shared with Edward over many dinners, discussing Auden's extraordinary life, prose, and poetry. Several letters, penned by W. H. Auden (copyright by the Estate of W. H. Auden), were allowed to be quoted herein.

I wish to thank my editors at Church Publishing Incorporated, Nancy Bryan and Milton Brasher-Cunningham, for their goodwill, professionalism, and considerable skills in enhancing the quality and appeal of this book.

By recognizing a long time ago the story's intrinsic pertinence, my wife, Freda, has had good reason to anticipate the book's completion, and toward that end, she has invigorated each step of the way, whether research or composition. Freda has read and commented on much of the text, offering wisdom and valuable criticism, and this book and I have been the resultant beneficiaries.

Explanatory Note

I N THE INITIAL PRAYER BOOK for the Church of England, Thomas Cranmer did not include a Psalter, but he incorporated the use of psalms at various points of worship with the presumption that Miles Coverdale's Great Bible of 1540 would be employed for the Book of Common Prayer of 1549—after all, the 1540 edition of the Great Bible contained a preface written by Thomas Cranmer. And yet, he did not bind those psalms within the original prayer book. The 1662 version of the Book of Common Prayer was the first to include psalms within the bounds of the book itself.

The current edition of the prayer book of the Episcopal Church, initially published in 1979, has allowed me to footnote, as appropriate, references to and specific language from the most recently retranslated psalms. However, the version of the psalms contained in the 1540 Great Bible is not of a nature to be readily relied upon for that purpose and footnoted in that fashion. While there is an underlying document in the form of the Great Bible, a comparison between the psalms of the 1979 Episcopal prayer book and those of the Great Bible would be virtually impossible without considerable adjustments being applied to the latter psalms to make them comprehensible to the present-day reader.

After spending a good deal of time with the psalms contained in Coverdale's 1540 Great Bible and with lines from the Book of Common Prayer of 1549 compiled by Cranmer, I have concluded it is much easier to read and decipher the words of Cranmer than those of Coverdale in the original forms of their respective books. Though the two documents were written within a few years of each other, Cranmer's texts are less burdened with the obstacles I find in Coverdale. I don't mean to devalue, in the least, the majestic beauty of the poetic style and rhythmic language of Coverdale's

retranslated psalms. Nevertheless, I do think W. H. Auden's asser-
tion that the presentation of the 1540 Great Bible psalms in their
original sixteenth-century form—with Coverdale's occasionally
strange and more unfamiliar spellings and punctuations, combined
with his dependence on unusual symbols to represent a variety of
different possibilities—conveys pellucid and understandable lines
to the twentieth-century reader is simply not true, certainly not
without a suitable crib.

For a comparison with the 1979 retranslated psalms, I have felt
it necessary to alter Coverdale's 1540 retranslation of the psalms
in conformance with more modern spelling and punctuation
practices; at the same time, I reverted to a Coverdale characteristic and reinstated the word "which" at relevant points in place
of the nominative pronoun "who," invoked for adjusted versions
appearing relatively soon after the publication of the Great Bible,
including the King James Bible of 1611 and the Book of Common
Prayer of 1662. There are several online copies of Coverdale's
1540 Great Bible, but in most cases they constitute unadulterated
representations, meaning the verse lines are set forth as originally displayed, without any attempt at modernization of spelling
and punctuation and other changes to permit reasonable access
for current readership. As a result of the alterations made to the
underlying Coverdale text, there is no base document to serve the
specific purpose for reference and, in turn, for footnotes; nonetheless, comparisons do occur herein between the 1979 prayer
book Psalter and the psalms of the 1540 Great Bible with the
latter being adjusted, as discussed.

Based on my research, three critical documents that bear on
Auden, the Psalms, and Me likely reside in the public domain: the
Great Bible of 1540, the Book of Common Prayer of 1549, and the
Book of Common Prayer of 1979. There are various reasons this
conclusion can be reached. First, it is frequently expressed that the
Great Bible is in the public domain, relying, in part, on the propo-
sition that works created or published prior to the mid-nineteenth
century are preponderantly and currently in the public domain.

There can be exceptions, of course, but for the present situation it is generally accepted that the King James Bible itself, produced more than half a century after the 1540 Great Bible, is also, at this time, in the public domain. Second, there is an understanding that in most of the world, including the United States, older prayer books, such as the 1549 version, can be freely reproduced as they are out of copyright. Moreover, the nominal predecessor to the Episcopal Church, the Protestant Episcopal Church, ratified in 1789 the unfettered use in the United States of the Book of Common Prayer, with substantial portions derived from the 1549 prayer book, including a Scottish imperative, approximately six years after the Treaty of Paris in 1783 formally brought the American-British conflict to a close. The 1928 version of the Book of Common Prayer of the Protestant Episcopal Church relied on and reprinted the earlier 1789 ratification. Third, the Book of Common Prayer of 1979 was issued into the public domain by the Episcopal Church immediately upon publication.

An exception to the public domain construct and generality exists in the United Kingdom, where a last remnant exists for the Crown to hold a monopoly over the printing and publishing of the Book of Common Prayer; apparently, the rights to the prayer book there fall under a perpetual royal prerogative.

CHAPTER 1

❦

A Strange Introduction

A BUBBLY AND SLIGHTLY MERCURIAL twenty-three-year-old in the winter of 1968, I found myself living on 22nd Street near Second Avenue in New York City. Fresh from educational pursuits at Harvard College, I was fresher still from the Civil Rights Revolution of the American South, which, after "Freedom Summer," I decided to witness firsthand back home, including attendance at the University of Arkansas.

My initial settlement into the great City proved easier than I had anticipated, securing both a decent job and an acceptable studio apartment. I didn't know much about New York, though during my years at Harvard I had traveled there a couple of times with a close friend and classmate whose older sister lived in the center of Manhattan. I somehow knew—even years before any attempt at the City—I would feel more at home in New York than I would in a place like Boston, which seemed at the time more set in its ways and less tolerant of those who needed, through much trial and probably much error, to rely on unconventional and self-styled ways of getting to the place where they wanted to go, wherever that was.

I loved poetry. I loved the idea of poetry. I loved my poetry. I loved other poets' poetry, especially W. H. Auden's poetry. One weekend afternoon soon after my arrival in New York, while doing nothing turned into doing something, I found myself thumbing through the City's gargantuan telephone book, starting with the letter "A," randomly scanning names—every kind of name of every

1

kind of spelling that began with "A." Whether by subconscious navigation, subtle discipline, or pure peculiarity, I stopped right on the name, "W. H. Auden." An unearthing of a poet, perhaps? Of course not. The eminent poet would not be so transparent or so foolishly democratic to list himself in the Manhattan phone book for everyone to see. I assumed it was just a duplicate name in a mammoth city.

But how could I drop my inquiry, now unanswered? How could I close the book and walk away without knowing? What if it were W. H. Auden who answered an envisioned phone call? The quest couldn't end here—even for a mere afternoon whimsy. What could he possibly do—yell at me? It probably wasn't him, in any case. I yet decided to proceed with a call, riding long distance on the hubris of the young. Someone picked up the phone, and I began to inquire:

"Is this W. H. Auden?"

"Yes."

"Is this the poet, W. H. Auden?"

"Yes."

It couldn't be, could it? Now, what to do? I started to stumble and stutter into some unrehearsed migration toward my admiration for and enjoyment of his verse. I remember his sort of chuckling; he immediately made me feel at ease, and we talked for awhile. I didn't feel at all rushed to hop off the call. What a strange onset. Three years later, as Auden's replacement on the drafting committee for the retranslation of the psalms contained in the Book of Common Prayer of the Episcopal Church, I'd be communicating with him and receiving letters from him on weighty matters of liturgy and liturgical vocabulary that bore on important theological and historical concerns. During our interchanges, I never once mentioned to Auden my capricious and solicitous Saturday afternoon phone call.

• • •

More than forty years later, I attended a lecture in 2012 on W. H. Auden, given by the Pulitzer Prize–winning poet Vijay Seshadri, at

Poets House in lower Manhattan. At the conclusion of the lecture, I joined a small dinner for Vijay, where I was seated next to David Lehman, the poet, editor, and anthologist. David and I spent the first part of dinner in a discussion over fedora hats, discovering quickly we were both hat people. I learned long ago that the world divides quite unevenly between hat and non-hat people, with there being notably many more non-hat people with whom we hat people have to contend. He and I then later ventured into an extensive conversation about Auden, for we both recognized we had not only fedora hats in common, but also a keen appreciation and admiration for the great poet. David ruminated about the topics the three of us would have possibly explored if Auden had been alive, sitting next to us; I suggested those subjects would have depended on his age at the time he joined us, hinting that few people, even in the literary world, were aware of Auden's intellectual and emotional engagement during the last years of his life in the revision of the Book of Common Prayer. I described Auden's participation on the drafting committee for the retranslation of the psalms, my replacement of Auden in 1971 (two years before his death) as the poet on the drafting committee when Auden decided to return to live in England, and the various communications he and I had on the project and related issues. By the time the dinner party ended, David had asked me to write an article for the Best American Poetry blog on my work with Auden in the retranslation of the psalms for the Episcopal Church.

In September 2012, the article "On Working with W. H. Auden on the Psalms" appeared on the Best American Poetry blog.[1] As a result of the piece, I received numerous direct communications from writers and poets. In most instances, their comments and inquiries reflected that few respondents were aware of Auden's focus, during his final years, on the psalms and the Book of Common Prayer. Several days following the article's distribution,

---

1. J. Chester Johnson, "On Working with W. H. Auden on the Psalms," Best American Poetry blog, September 17, 2012.

my wife and I had dinner with Edward Mendelson and his wife, Cheryl. Edward, who is Auden's literary executor and principal biographer, decided to end his latest biography of the poet, *Later Auden*, published in 1999, with reference to letters from Auden to me on the Psalter revision and a discussion of Auden's involvement in and attitude toward the revision of the entire Book of Common Prayer.[2] Edward, who brought his own copy of the Book of Common Prayer to dinner, began to ask me to clarify and supplement parts of my article. As a result of the many inquisitive responses to my first piece, I decided to write a second article that dealt with some of the comments and inquiries. In October 2012, "Auden on Prayer Book Revision: No More Mr. Nice Guy?" appeared on the Best American Poetry blog.[3]

New attention followed the second piece, resulting in a much longer article, "Auden: Defender at Dusk," on an associated topic for the book *W. H. Auden: Quaderns de Versalia*, published in Spain and in Spanish, with an English version of that article appearing in the United States at the end of 2014 in the literary journal, *Green Mountains Review*. Most recently, in June 2015, an extensive interview with me, "After Auden: Retranslating the Psalms," was published in the literary journal, *Illuminations*.

Auden, the Psalms, and Me will now finish a story cycle, found of ancient poems, Elizabethan English, a very famous poet, and an immense struggle to reconcile time, eternity, and word.

---

2. Edward Mendelson, *Later Auden* (New York: Farrar, Straus and Giroux, 1999), 518–19.

3. J. Chester Johnson, "Auden on Prayer Book Revision: No More Mr. Nice Guy?," Best American Poetry blog, October 8, 2012.

CHAPTER 2

༄

Without Warning

LTHOUGH REARED A METHODIST in the Bible Belt on the cusp of the Mississippi River Delta in rural southeast Arkansas, I nevertheless developed an early abiding affection and affinity for the Book of Common Prayer. Maybe it was simply the association many English poets had with this special book of worship; yet, in truth, I am certain it was more than that. I gravitated to its elevated language and its ability to capture the ineffable at the sharp angles of its literary perspective—its prayers, its poetry, its Psalter. The Methodist Church and the Episcopal Church in the United States share numerous common roots, including reliance at a point in time on the contents of a previous Anglican prayer book, and the two organizations actually considered a merger in the early 1790s.[1] So it would not be surprising that a less than fully conceded, indefinite gravitation emerged in me over time to the words of the Episcopal prayer book.

In early 1971, still technically a Methodist but living in New York City and attending an Episcopal church, I had the good fortune of reading a series of "draft psalms" that had been prepared by the drafting committee for the retranslation of the Episcopal psalms; as I learned, the retranslation represented only part of the entire revision of the Book of Common Prayer that had been formally underway for about three years. I was exhilarated; of course,

---

1. Robert W. Prichard, *A History of the Episcopal Church* (New York: Morehouse Publishing, 2014), 125.

I knew about the mistranslations in the Coverdale version of the psalms as part of the prayer book, recalling the words of C. S. Lewis that "a sound modern scholar has more Hebrew in his little finger than poor Coverdale had in his whole body,"[2] and I knew about the stodginess of some of the language; but to think of a new retranslation, drawing on the best of the old, but incorporating the more accurate (hence, more truthful) words and scholarship and more forthright and informal texture through current usage of the English/American language—now that was a project worth exploring.

With the exaggerated certitude only the young possess, ply, and inflict on older types, I immediately sat down and dashed off letters to key members of the drafting committee, discussing my endorsement of the Psalter retranslation project (as though they needed it). Among those on the committee to whom I wrote were Reverend Canon Charles M. Guilbert, chair of the committee and custodian of the Book of Common Prayer; the poet, W. H. Auden; and Dr. Robert C. Dentan, the notable Old Testament scholar and professor at General Theological Seminary, who had also sat on a similar committee for the Revised Standard Version of the Bible. In my note, I referred to my commitment to verse, my work as a poet, and my respect and affection for the psalms. I also mentioned my own translation endeavors, including recent efforts with poet and translator Jean Starr Untermeyer, rather well known at the time, who had been married a couple of times to the poet and anthologist Louis Untermeyer. The editor of a literary journal that had published both my verse and several poems translated by her arranged for Jean and me to meet in New York City, and the two of us, though generations apart in age, thereafter labored together on a series of poetry translations.

I understood there were three hundred consultants to the revision program for the Book of Common Prayer. Perhaps the Episcopal Church could fit some young blood—namely mine—among

---

2. C. S. Lewis, *Reflections on the Psalms* (New York: Harcourt, 1986), 7.

those consultants. I certainly didn't expect such an unreal possibility to materialize, but I did fantasize about it. Of course, my note had gratuitously offered my services and talents. I even pondered that the drafting committee might pass along their drafts of the psalms, and I would offer ideas for consideration.

To my surprise, I received replies from everyone I penned. Auden's letter was short, but cordial. He believed his role was to effect the continued retention of the Coverdale retranslation of the Psalter unless there were mistranslations. Coverdale had been substantially maintained in the then current version of the Book of Common Prayer. Of particular import was the reply from Canon Guilbert, who invited me to his office in New York City to discuss the project.[3] Before the end of a long session with Canon Guilbert conversing about poetry, the psalms, retranslating techniques, and more, I was asked to join the drafting committee. Soon thereafter, I also became a member of the Episcopal Church. Today, I am one of only two surviving members of the committee.

Auden had decided to relocate to England for his winter home and would consequently no longer be available. As a result, the drafting committee lacked a poet. As fortune would have it, my inquiring letter could not have been timelier or more serendipitous.

Once a member of the drafting committee at the grand old age of twenty-six, being at least twenty years younger than the next youngest member, I had some second, foreboding thoughts. Maybe I had been too quick to write a letter offering my meager talents and experience; maybe I had let the mettle of my youth take unbridled control of my interest and zeal for the project. Over forty years later, I can still remember my first meeting with members of the committee, sans Auden, over dinner at the General Theological Seminary in the Chelsea section of Manhattan. At that point, I hardly remained a gushing force of hubris—it was now simply a matter of survival. Yes, of course, the sample psalms from the committee I

---

3. Letter to J. Chester Johnson from Canon Charles M. Guilbert, dated January 27, 1971. Courtesy of the Archives of the Episcopal Church.

had perused needed a hand of poetics applied more proactively and constantly, but had I been the right choice? That first night, I mumbled my way through the session, eagerly anticipating a liberating cessation to the evening's work, so I could regroup, repair any damage, reconstruct, and reemerge—I needed directional bearings. The work finally ended for the night with a social hour with exhortatory conversation and goodwill (and excellent scotch, I might add) that reinforced the reason for my being there and led to sleeplessness found of my anticipation for the morning's gathering. Over time, I came to the irreverent and immodest conclusion that I had indeed been a good selection for no other reason than the uncompromising commitment I had made to this effort of retranslating the psalms for the Book of Common Prayer.

Notwithstanding his departure from the committee, Auden voiced through mail to me his opinion about how the retranslation process for the Psalter should be pursued and, more strongly, how the revision program for the entire Book of Common Prayer should be arranged. A question still lingered, however: Who did Canon Guilbert really want to replace W. H. Auden? I've often pondered that question. Clearly, there were many more credentialed than I who could have stepped into Auden's place. In the end, I've reached several conclusions. First, at our meeting that followed my initial written inquiry, I think Canon Guilbert decided he could work with me; it doubtlessly had been a rather rapid decision on his part—I'm sure he settled on me right then and there. Second, my youth and energy appealed to him; much remained to be done with the psalms, and he responded favorably to my rather untempered fervor about the retranslation. I never missed a meeting once appointed to the committee. Third, Auden's schedule, prestige, and demands had various minuses: he was away for the summer in Austria, and when not there, his travel schedule in the United States and elsewhere often conflicted with meeting dates for the committee. Canon Guilbert wanted someone close at hand. Indeed, in his January 27, 1971 letter extending an invitation for our original meeting, Guilbert had written:

As you may know, W. H. Auden is a member of the Committee. However, he is in Austria from April to October, and has a heavy lecture schedule when he is in the States, so that for too many of our sessions we have been without the advice and counsel of a poet.[4]

Fourth, I later learned from other committee members that Guilbert and Auden often argued about the nature of and need for changes to Coverdale's words and phrases, reflective, in part, of Auden's refractory attitude toward any changes at all, except for demonstratively egregious ones. Guilbert saw in me someone willing to consider a new approach to traditional, if not codified, idiom. While the presence of W. H. Auden carried enormous weight with parties and persons inside and outside of the Episcopal Church, Guilbert needed a workhorse to participate as a poet on the committee. After publication of the new Episcopal Book of Common Prayer in 1979, I received an individual citation from the Standing Liturgical Commission, which oversaw the revisions for the new prayer book. The essential elements of the citation read:

> The Standing Liturgical Commission of the Episcopal Church and its Committee for the Revision of the Prayer Book Psalter record their profound appreciation of the contribution of J. Chester Johnson to their work . . . his marked poetic gifts for words and sounds and rhythms, his diligent labors in comparing other modern versions of the Psalms, and his quiet and sensitive spiritual insights have enriched the lives of his colleagues and helped to shape the final text of the Psalter as it now appears in the Book of Common Prayer for 1979.[5]

Once I was appointed to the committee, Canon Guilbert and I worked closely together over the next few years. We actually

---

4. Ibid.
5. Citation from the Standing Liturgical Commission of the Episcopal Church, December 1979.

became quite good friends. He also was a mentor to me for years, even following the completion of the revised Psalter, so much so that I named my only son after him. Away from committee meetings, we often shared meals and discussed issues affecting the retranslation generally and individual psalms to be considered at forthcoming sessions. With expertise and facility in each of the relevant languages, Guilbert routinely issued a draft of the psalms to be considered in advance of the next meeting; the sessions, held over several days, were normally convened twice a year, either at the General Theological Seminary or at the National Episcopal Church Center, both in New York City. Soon after my appointment, I provided members, prior to our sessions, with spreadsheet comparisons for individual verse lines from numerous, recent, and well-respected translations of those psalms we were scheduled to retranslate. I continued to furnish this material for each session through the remaining life of the committee. I applied a special eye for verse formulations contained in those other versions. The committee members, who worked independently during the months between our meetings, relied most heavily on Canon Guilbert's drafts as the starting point for our discussions. We made frequent adjustments to the texture, fluidity, and poetic nature of his draft language, and examined the scholarship and poetic approach taken by the other translations I provided. This latter resource helped to confirm our decisions, if not open prospects for debate and additional exploration. The Psalter retranslation project, which started in earnest about 1968, lasted until final publication in 1979.

It would ostensibly seem that a true rendering of the meaning of the considered text should, as a matter of practice and principle, have to precede any contributions by a poet. However, I often drew questions from the scholars about alternative language to that which had been used in previous retranslations of individual psalms that bore on those within the Episcopal Book of Common Prayer. In this respect, the scholars found it necessary to determine whether mistranslations surfaced at points along the trail of the "received text" over the many centuries—from the original Hebrew through the Greek (Septuagint), through Old Latin, and through Jerome's Vulgate Latin revision to Miles Coverdale's sixteenth-century retranslation, which also relied, in part, on Luther's German Bible. Of course, as either a member of the drafting committee or a reader or reciter of these ancient poems, we all prefer to know that the lines originally translated or subsequently retranslated through the ages represented the true text; otherwise, we might as well take the psalms as they appear in the Book of Common Prayer as being no more than the farcical or whimsical. One final step for the committee would involve a review of the 1928 version of the Book of Common Prayer, which had accomplished a number of adjustments to the inherited Psalter. Thus, the poet's role was not isolated to only the final phase once the true meaning had been clearly established; rather, the interplay was more iterative with participation by the poet occurring even in the midst of verification of meaning for the much earlier and organic versions.

While an overlap of a few months existed between Auden's participation and my own, we never attended the same Psalter committee meeting. As a result, I cannot be a firsthand source for Auden's textual offerings to the finally adopted retranslation. The question has been posed to me many times over the years: How much was W. H. Auden truly involved in the retranslation of the psalms? I should note that he was a member of the drafting committee for some time before I arrived, so it would simply not be possible for me to give comprehensive and detailed insight into all of his poetic offerings to our retranslation. Nonetheless, I did serve with earnest attention and participation on the committee from 1971 to 1979—most of the life of the project—so I have a solid knowledge of its history, even for the period in advance of my actual membership. In chapter seven, I examine various views, expressed by W. H. Auden, toward the retranslation of the psalms, as a general matter, and toward appropriate language changes for certain individual psalms. An ambivalence surrounded Auden's participation in the retranslation project. On the one hand, he realized that glaring mistranslations existed in the Miles Coverdale psalms for the 1549 prayer book that had been carried forward in succeeding Psalters. On the other, he opposed any wholesale revision to the Book of Common Prayer, a position I came to realize he had voiced powerfully from time to time. His frustration pullulating between what was actually happening in the Episcopal Church and his countervailing beliefs caused him to back away from liturgical practices to which he had been aligned for many years. The last communication Auden held with the drafting committee—written after he no longer served—came by way of an extraordinary letter he sent to me during the summer of 1971, to which I will now turn.

W. H. Auden and the Letter of July 6, 1971

OVER THE YEARS, it has been somewhat astounding that so few people were aware of W. H. Auden's intense and full engagement in the Episcopal Church's revision of the Book of Common Prayer, begun during the late 1960s. His most intense response to the endeavor dealt with matters away from the revision of the psalms, while his principal, personal involvement consisted of his role for about three years as poet on the drafting committee for the retranslation of the Psalter.

Even though Auden viewed his participation in the overall revision of the Book of Common Prayer ambivalently, the project, including both the entire scope of the book's revision and his specific work on the retranslation of the psalms, nevertheless occupied a good deal of his attention and remained central to him during this period, as evidenced by the number and intensity of letters and other pieces he wrote around that time. Edward Mendelson, Auden's literary executor and principal biographer, suggests at the closing of the biography, *Later Auden*, that the following attitude drove W. H. Auden's frame of mind toward the poet's role in and reactions to the revision project:

> On the subjects that mattered most, the loud familiar language
> of the present day was likely to confirm one's private interests

and prejudices, while the quiet distant languages of the past might perhaps overthrow them.[1]

Auden's views on the revision of the psalms focused on protection of the verse, as illustrated in one letter to me: "All I can do is to try to persuade the scholars not to alter Coverdale unless there is a definite mistranslation."[2] To him, if there were to be a revision to the original sixteenth-century Anglican retranslation by Miles Coverdale, then his mission was to make sure the surgery on his beloved psalms happened tenderly. At the same time, his riposte toward certain, non-Psalter changes to the Book of Common Prayer was surely not so well-mannered.

Whenever Auden refers to the Coverdale psalms, we can assume he means the version included in the 1928 Episcopal Book of Common Prayer, which carries them mostly undiminished, except mainly for more current spelling and punctuation modifications. Similarly, we can assume the same whenever Auden comments on the Book of Common Prayer generally, although he is also probably thinking of lines he learned and memorized from the 1662 version as a young choirboy in England.

In July 1971, I received a letter from W. H. Auden—postmarked Kirchstetten, Austria, his summer home—after my appointment to replace him as the poet on the drafting committee. Later I came to realize this letter proved to be Auden's valediction from his work on the retranslation of the psalms. At the time of writing the letter, Auden, then in the process of making arrangements to move permanently from his winter home of New York City back to Britain, did not expect to be available any longer to assist in the retranslation project; he had tired of the City and was returning to the country of his birth, his education, and his early success as a poet and person of letters.

---

1. Mendelson, *Later Auden*, 518.
2. Letter to J. Chester Johnson from W. H. Auden, dated January 28, 1971.

Ju y 6th, I97I

3062 KIRCHSTETTEN
BEZ. ST. PÖLTEN
HINTERHOLZ 6
N.-Ö. AUSTRIA

Dear Mr Johnson:

Thank you for your letter. What has happened over the last few years has made me realise that those who rioted when Cranmer introduced a venacular liturgy were right. When this reform nonsense started, what we should have done is the exact opposite of the Roman Catholics: we should have said"Henceforth,we will have the Book of Common Prayer in Latin. (There happens to be an excellent translation.)

In my view,the Rite - preaching,of course,is another matter - is the link between the dead and the unborn. This calls for a timeless language which,in practice,means a dead language.

My own parish church has gone so crazy that I have to go to the Russian Orthodox church where,thank God,though I know what is going on,I don't understand a single word.

The odd thing about the Liturgical Reform movement is that,it is not asked for by the laity - they dislike ite it is a fad of a few crazy priests. If they imagine that their high-jinks will bring youth into the churches,they are very much mistaken.

As for the Psalms,they are poems,and to'get' poetry,it should, of course,be read in the language in which it was written. I myself, alas,know no Hebrew. All I know is that Coverdale reads like poetry, and the modern versions don't.

Lastly,I don't believe there is such an animal as Twentieth Kentury Man.

with best wishes

Yours sincerely

W.H.Auden

The Auden letter, which centered on the liturgical reforms and the revisions to the Book of Common Prayer, constituted more than a mere remonstration. It was impassioned and far-reaching with learned assumptions and unconventional propositions involving "the Rite" (his nomenclature for the Eucharist), which he described in the letter as being the "link between the dead and the unborn," and the usefulness of employing "a dead language" in the form of Latin for "the Rite" and for the Book of Common Prayer collectively. He also excoriated the "high-jinks," as he put it, being perpetrated by the Episcopal priests through the liturgical revamping program, inciting him to refuse attendance at his own neighborhood Episcopal church in favor of a Russian Orthodox church, where he couldn't "understand a single word."[3]

3. Letter to J. Chester Johnson from W. H. Auden, dated July 6, 1971.

By the summer of 1971, Auden had obviously become more than a little annoyed with the entire Episcopal liturgical reform movement. Looking at the verse in Auden's final two volumes of poetry—*Epistle to a Godson and Other Poems* and *Thank You, Fog*—with an eye for any poems that reflected his attitude toward the Book of Common Prayer, it seems only fitting this quatrain appeared in the poem "Doggerel by a Senior Citizen" from *Epistle to a Godson and Other Poems*, published in 1972:

> The Book of Common Prayer we knew
> Was that of 1662:
> Though with-it sermons may be well,
> Liturgical reforms are hell.[4]

Also, this excerpt from the poem "Address to the Beasts," included in *Thank You, Fog*, published posthumously in 1974, probably even more effectively confirmed his irritation:

> . . . and, though unconscious of God,
> your sung Eucharists are
> more hallowed than ours.[5]

So, how engaged was Auden in the revision of the Book of Common Prayer and in the related retranslation of the psalms? He wrote to the chairman of the Psalter retranslation project, penned other letters and at least one article, and contributed in a notable way to the retranslation, which was published in 1979 in the revised prayer book, presently being used by Episcopal churches throughout the United States. Moreover, the psalms on which Auden and I worked were adopted for worship books and services by certain other denominations and by other branches of the Anglican Communion, which we will discuss a little later.

---

4. W. H. Auden, "Doggerel by a Senior Citizen," in *Epistle to a Godson and Other Poems* (New York: Random House, 1972), 35.

5. W. H. Auden, "Address to the Beasts," in *Thank You, Fog* (New York: Random House, 1974), 13.

Auden's July 1971 letter speaks for itself in terms of personal encounter toward the end of his days, at the "dusk" of his daylight. He died a little more than two years later in September 1973. Here was a preeminent American-English poet—perhaps, the preeminent poet of the English language for the twentieth century—sending a letter of consequential thinking and spiritual reflection to a twenty-something poet who had no professional name to speak of and whose only nexus with him consisted of our roles in the retranslation of the psalms. We exchanged letters three times on subjects dealing with the project; his written responses on two such occasions being cordial, but largely perfunctory. The July 1971 reply was far different. This one had a mission, a purpose. Why me? I have my suspicions. He presumed, I believe, that I would likely be involved in the Psalter retranslation project to its very completion (which I was—to final publication), and, as a result of my age, be witness to the overall liturgical reform program of the Episcopal Church for years to come. He wanted the subsequent generation to know his attitude and reservations.

Edward Mendelson and Arthur Kirsch, both of whom have brought substantive insight to the religious and spiritual focus in Auden's writings, are clear exceptions to my criticism that literary commentators often miss a good deal of Auden by paying too little attention to the pervasive theological underpinnings of his poetic art and voice. A couple of reasons can explain this avoidance. First, a tendency at present exists to eschew the relationship between Auden's faith and his poetic composition, for the word "religion" and the term "Christianity" regularly carry an air of fustiness and superannuation in literary quarters. Second, there is often a conspicuous lack of familiarity with the language and related history that characterized Auden's religious and spiritual convictions and theology—his devotion, if you will. Should one therefore be devoid of a grasp of certain essential history and language, illustrative of Auden's reliance on religious and spiritual "reason," then it is surely much better to leave things unsaid and abandon the subject, mostly untouched. However, it is, I think, impossible to understand much of Auden's poetry without an appreciation for this faithful and worshipful element of his life and work. Ironically, he described a somewhat analogous situation in *Forewords and Afterwords* when explaining the theological language of the Catholic mystics and the prospects for misunderstanding the meaning of some of their writings without background in the context of their language and lives.[6] The same warning could be given, in some important respects, about W. H. Auden himself.

Over time, the meaning and message of the special Auden missive came into sharper focus as I learned more about his theological and liturgical inclinations and as I grew increasingly familiar with the effects of Charles Williams's beliefs and writings on Auden. The connection between Williams and the contents of the July 1971 letter eventually became rather evident. In fact, Auden gave voice in 1956 to this conclusion in the introduction to Williams's classic, *The Descent of the Dove*, which had originally appeared in 1939:

> I have been reading and rereading *The Descent of the Dove* for some sixteen years now and I find it a source of intellectual delight and spiritual nourishment which remains inexhaustible.[7]

It is rumored Auden read Williams's book annually. Apparently, Auden told friends he had met two saints during his lifetime, Charles Williams and Dorothy Day.[8] Arthur Kirsch mentions in *Auden and Christianity* that upon meeting Charles Williams in the late 1930s, Auden remarked, ". . . for the first time in my life I felt myself in the presence of personal sanctity."[9] Williams, twenty years senior to Auden, died in 1945.

In *The Descent of the Dove*, Charles Williams refers to "the Rite" as the Eucharist Food—elements of bread and wine served

---

6. W. H. Auden, "The Protestant Mystics," in *Forewords and Afterwords* (New York: Random House, 1973), 76.

7. W. H. Auden, "Introduction to *The Descent of the Dove* by Charles Williams," in *The Complete Works of W. H. Auden Prose, Volume IV, 1956–1962* (Princeton, NJ: Princeton University Press, 2010), 30.

8. David Garrett Izzo, *W. H. Auden Encyclopedia* (Jefferson, NC: McFarland & Co., 2010), 65.

9. Arthur Kirsch, *Auden and Christianity* (New Haven: Yale University Press, 2005), 23.

to Christian congregations for a sharing (in a spiritual sense or by transubstantiation) of the body and blood of Christ. It is to this term and meaning that Auden returns in his use of "the Rite" in the July 1971 letter as "the link between the dead and the unborn."[10] He had made use of a similar phrase in his introduction to *The Descent of the Dove*—"the already dead and the as yet unborn"— alluding to requisite regard not being limited to those souls who just happen to live in one's own time.[11] Williams previously made the judgment that "the great Rite soared to its climax in the eternal, and yet communicated the eternal to time." Williams expanded this Eucharistic thought by quoting the words of Gregory the Great:

> [T]hings lowest are brought into communion with the highest, things earthly are united with the heavenly, and the things that are seen and those which are unseen become one. . . . History and contemporaneity and futurity were joined.[12]

Auden proposed in the letter that rather than completing its planned prayer book revision, the Episcopal Church "should have said 'Henceforth, we will have the Book of Common Prayer in Latin.'" Because Latin constitutes a "dead language," it would also serve the purpose of satisfying Auden's criterion as a language for "the Rite" in linking "the dead and the unborn" and thereby additionally reducing the problem of time in eternity that has historically plagued Christianity.[13] Both Auden and Williams shared a recognition that Christianity traditionally faced a significant tension, if not a conundrum, with time in eternity. Time depended on eternity, or, as Williams had also stated about this continuous stress, "Christianity was dealing on one side with temporal and on the other with eternal affairs, but it was one Christendom."[14]

---

10. Letter to J. Chester Johnson from W. H. Auden, dated July 6, 1971.

11. Auden, "Introduction to *The Descent of the Dove* by Charles Williams," 26.

12. Charles Williams, *The Descent of the Dove* (Vancouver: Regent College Publishing, 2002), 114–15.

13. Letter to J. Chester Johnson from W. H. Auden, dated July 6, 1971.

14. Williams, *The Descent of the Dove*, 103.

Auden further refined the unreconciled nature of time in eternity in his *For the Time Being—A Christmas Oratorio* with the Chorus asking this question:

> How could the Eternal do a temporal act,
> The Infinite become a finite fact?[15]

In the same piece, the Narrator attempts a partial answer:

> . . . the Kingdom of Heaven may come, not in our present
> And not in our future, but in the Fullness of Time.[16]

Without getting into high weeds through too much deliberation on Christology, parousia, eschatology, and the like, it is reasonable to conclude Auden thought the expanded population (i.e., "the dead and the unborn") that he and Williams believed were incorporate in the Eucharist could help supply at least a partial reconciliation to the thorny issue of "time in eternity." To mitigate the complexity of "time in eternity," the necessity exists for time and eternity to move toward oneness. Thus, as stated in the July 1971 letter, Auden recommended that "the Rite" install a dead language: Latin. Beyond the fact it had ceased to be employed in any determinative, communal sense, there were certain other features about Latin that would have made it the preferred eucharistic form of communication. Williams espoused Latin as the principal language of the inherited faith, drawing much on the flight of Greek that occurred in the Western world, when Latin gained its inimitable and preemptive role for Christians. In addition, there was Latin's reliance on peasant rhythms, assonance, and folk-poetry. "The Faith had to talk Latin," Williams said in explaining the Christian Church's historically heavy dependence on the language.[17] It was logical, therefore, for Auden to name Latin the choice dead language for the institutionally sponsored Eucharist.

---

15. W. H. Auden, "For the Time Being," in *Collected Longer Poems* (New York: Random House, 1969), 138.

16. Ibid, 163.

17. Williams, *The Descent of the Dove*, 78.

In his own poems and writings, Auden often pushed and enlarged the parameters of word meanings and usage. He routinely examined old, if not ancient, employment of individual words to justify unusual word forms. In turn, however, Auden did not appear to have any problem embracing neologisms Williams enlisted to empower and clarify particular theological points. One obvious example is the word "co-inherence" and its verb "co-inhere." To Williams, the concept meant to have or to share inherent aspects of one another, to reflect as scripturally, "He in us and we in him." Toward unity—whether in the disposition of a dead language for capturing the expanded populations of the "dead and the unborn," or in the linkage of time and eternity becoming more closely aligned through Latin or in the combination of body, blood, and spirit through celebration of the Eucharist— Auden could accept and apply Williams's term, "co-inherence." The term also coincided well with Auden's own personal experience with and attitude toward the Christian concept of agape love, that multiple love, that love shared with other humans, the love that Auden had said was expressed to him one summer night in June 1933, when he considered himself on the verge of being "done with Christianity for good." Sitting on a lawn with three colleagues, he felt invaded by a power that was irresistible and not his own, and he then knew exactly "what it means to love one's neighbor as oneself."[18]

The co-inherence construct extended beyond the incarnational between God and human to the broad human community in the form of "the City," which emerged in Williams's book *The Image of the City*. The name of "the City" to Williams was Union, and any exclusion from "the City" became hell: "[I]t is the doctrine that no man lives to himself or indeed *from* himself. . . . We are, simply, utterly dependent on others."[19] "Bear ye one another's burdens."[20]

---

18. Auden, *Forewords and Afterwords*, 69.

19. Charles Williams, *The Image of the City* (Berkeley: Apocryphile Press, 2007), 103–5.

20. Anne Ridler, Introduction to *The Image of the City* by Charles Williams (Berkeley: Apocryphile Press, 2007), xlvii.

C. S. Lewis, a fellow member of the "Inklings" along with Williams and J. R. R. Tolkien, once said of Williams:

> On many of us the prevailing impression made by the London streets is one of chaos; but Williams, looking on the same spectacle, saw chiefly an image—an imperfect, pathetic, heroic, and majestic image—of Order.[21]

After World War II, Auden didn't quite apprehend "the City" the same way Williams had. In "Memorial for the City," which Auden composed "In memoriam Charles Williams, d. April 1945," he contended:

> Sundered by reason and treason the City
> Found invisible ground for concord in measured sound,
>   While wood and stone learned the shameless
> Games of man, to flatter, to show off, be pompous, to romp.[22]

And, yet, more than two decades later, Auden, imagining the holy, human city, seized more fully Williams's stance, enlisting the neologism, co-inhering, in the poem "United Nations Hymn," contained in *Epistle to a Godson and Other Poems*:

> . . . Not interfering
> But co-inhering,
> For all within
> The cincture of the sound
> Is holy ground,
> Where all are Brothers,
> None faceless Others.[23]

Little did I realize over forty years ago when I started to work on the retranslation of the psalms that, in a small, but acute and virtually

---

21. Ibid.

22. W. H. Auden, "Memorial for the City," in *Collected Shorter Poems, 1927–1957* (New York: Random House, 1967), 291.

23. Auden, *Epistle to a Godson and Other Poems*, 63.

orphic manner, my life would unwittingly be tied to W. H. Auden. I long ago lost count of the many times I've been asked about him as a result of our respective work, though many of those inquiries had absolutely nothing to do with the project. This association with Auden caused me to learn much more about him than I otherwise would have, and that process has had its pleasurable and meaning-ful impacts. Once, I remarked to a friend that the association with Auden had meant not just getting to know his work and life better but also getting to know his friends and the influences, mirrored in the realms of literature, literary criticism, and theology. Charles Wil-liams proved to be one of the more fascinating and visionary of those friends and influences. The July 6, 1971 letter impelled me forward into an Auden world where he stood embattled at the gates with his confrere in arms, Charles Williams (though then perished, but still whispering and encouraging), against marauding Visigoths who were, to Auden, prepared to vanquish the citadel of the Word—the literary, spiritual, and theological Word. It is not surprising that at Auden's dusk, he would choose Williams to share, to "co-inhere," if you will, in a final defense.

Notwithstanding the deep reservations Auden held about the general revisions to the Book of Common Prayer, he felt compelled to offer help, reflecting his considerable ties to the institution of the Episcopal Church. At one point, as we will discuss further in a different context, Auden wrote to Guilbert stating his willingness to serve in any capacity on the Standing Liturgical Commission.[24] We will return to the correspondence between Auden and Guilbert in chapter seven. I believe this offer to assist illustrated a genuine generosity and goodwill, which do not comport with the judgment, among many people, that W. H. Auden regularly exhibited a honed attitude of curmudgeonliness in his later years. My interchanges with and knowledge of him cannot confirm the latter view. A per-son of strong ideas he was, with polymathic knowledge and precise

---

24. Letter to Canon Guilbert from W. H. Auden, dated December 22, 1967. Courtesy of the Archives of the Episcopal Church.

proportion at his fingertips to enhance and justify his views, but he was mostly accessible and transparent, not rude, arrogant, or routinely short—not from my experience.

There is also a story involving Edward Mendelson that corresponds with my own recollections. These remembrances offer countervailing testimony to those who suggest that Auden, as a practice, exercised brief tolerance and quick severity. Mendelson authorized me to relay this story, which apparently had not previously appeared in the public arena, for one of my 2012 articles on the Best American Poetry blog; the story is repeated here. Mendelson was an assistant professor at Yale when given the job of serving as Auden's chaperon and guide on a visit the poet made to the campus to talk with students and to record his poems. During the stay, Auden mentioned to Mendelson that he wanted to put together a new collection of his essays, to be titled *Forewords and Afterwords*. Auden didn't remember, however, what he had written, to which Mendelson replied that he, Mendelson, had copied all of Auden's essays, which were then in Mendelson's apartment. Auden, obviously pleased, spent a few hours with the copies but then said he would need to return at a later date in order to read all of the essays. Following the trip to Yale and after Auden had announced a trip to England, he wrote and asked Mendelson to make the selections and included a check for $150 to cover the costs of copying. In turn, Mendelson put together a preliminary list of contents, which Auden reviewed and amended. A few days later, Mendelson sent a sheaf of copies to Auden. Sometime after these exchanges, Auden then asked Mendelson to be his literary executor, and still later, Mendelson remitted a check to Auden for $40, the sum remaining after the costs of copying and mailing were paid for the *Forewords and Afterwords* project. When Auden received the check, it is reported that there ensued a moment of jovial celebration for Auden and his partner, Chester Kallman, with much waving of the check, for, as then exclaimed, they had, at last, found an honest man.[25]

---

25. Johnson, "Auden on Prayer Book Revision: No More Mr. Nice Guy?", October 8, 2012.

CHAPTER 4

◦◦

Psalms as Poetry

W E SHOULD REMEMBER the psalms are and were, in their initial compositions, poems—with the entirety of the Psalter (all one hundred and fifty of them) being merely a congeries of individual poems or simply a volume of verse. Of course, these psalms have been used extensively in liturgical practices, but they are still poems. Many of them are often highly cherished not only among those who regularly read and sing them in worship services, but also by the general public and non-religious folk as well. In the words of the British writer C. S. Lewis,

> Most emphatically the Psalms must be read as poems; as lyrics, with all the licences and all the formalities, the hyperboles, the emotional rather than logical connections, which are proper to lyric poetry. They must be read as poems if they are to be understood; no less than French must be read as French or English as English. Otherwise we shall miss what is in them and think we see what is not.[1]

Many people who do not darken the door of a house of worship can often recite substantial portions of individual psalms, reflecting their poetic, literary value outside of liturgical use.

The one hundred and fifty poems constituting the Psalter have engendered admiration, emulation, and enduring precedent for a long line of English and American poets. Like so many of those

---

1. Lewis, *Reflections on the Psalms*, 3.

poets before and after him, W. H. Auden regarded the psalms as a special body of memorable poetry. Aligned with Auden's predilection to honor these pieces as poems, it is obvious that we should see the Psalter itself as an entire body of poetry. In fact, one could argue convincingly that the Psalter has been the most influential body or book of poems in the Western world. Certainly, the beauty, eloquence, and the literary devices of parallelism, rhetoric, imagery, cadence, and hyperbole, among others, captured in the psalms and broadly disseminated throughout the Judeo-Christian consciousness have constantly stood at the shoulders of Western poets. It seems to me that to characterize the psalms "pre-literary," as some have, meaning their existence preceded literature, while, at the same time, admitting to their eminent influence on poetry over three millennia, borders on the self-contradictory. While the form of the psalms evolved through our language into different applications, their original construction influenced the direction of our own verse. For example, though the ancient Hebrew ear apparently relished more truncated lines and fewer cadences, the English-American ear, as a general matter, extrapolated verse structure into longer lines and more cadences. There are no dominant metrical patterns in the Psalter contained in the Book of Common Prayer; the lines are of varying length with varying numbers of syllables and a variety of rhythms. It should be emphasized that the poetry lines in the retranslated psalms that now appear in the Episcopal prayer book correspond to Hebrew verse, which is not based on meter or rhyme, but on symmetry of form and impression, and often on parallelism of clauses, as illustrated in Psalm 93:4:

> The waters have lifted up, O LORD;
>> the waters have lifted up their voice;
>>> the waters have lifted up their pounding waves.

Or by contrast, as in Psalm 1:6:

> For the LORD knows the way of the righteous,
>> but the way of the wicked is doomed.

Or by extension of concept, as in Psalm 123:3:

> So our eyes look to the LORD our God,
> until he show us his mercy.[2]

As described elsewhere herein, the drafting committee decided to print the psalms as poetry, rather than as prose, which had frequently been done in previous prayer books. In this fashion, a couplet became the normal verse for the psalms, although triplets and quatrains appear now and then—the quatrains being mostly the combination of two couplets.

Notwithstanding many other adaptations, including major adjustments to subject matter and tone, the model of the psalms has persisted to effect a stylistic reference point among English and American writers of verse—in innumerable cases, no doubt, without the literary practitioner's conscious knowledge of the association.

Modern scholarship has advised that the first psalms, which eventually developed into a compendium of ancient religious poetry, began to be written around 1000 BCE, soon after David, the legendary warrior-leader-poet, forged Israel into a formidable theocracy. Scholars generally agree that the composition of the psalms then continued through the period that followed the rebuilding of the second temple in Jerusalem and ended sometime around or possibly even after 500 BCE. When the Hebrews returned from the Babylonian exile around 535 BCE, they renewed a commitment to the faith of their ancestors by taking a series of redemptive steps, including the codification of a worship book of psalms. So, we poets today reach back through three millennia to establish a connection with some early architects and engineers of our craft.

English and American poets have often focused their talents on adaptation of the psalms by having them become metrical and rhythmic for the English language, by using them for launching

---

2. Charles M. Guilbert, *The Psalter: A New Version for Public Worship and Private Devotion* (New York: Seabury Press, 1978), viii–ix.

related or derived insights, by imposing on them personal and stylistic characteristics and devices, or by retranslating them so the poems comport with up-to-date Hebrew scholarship. George Herbert's translation of Psalm 23, John Donne's poem upon the translation of the psalms by Philip and Mary Sidney, and the Sidneys' own psalm adaptations stand as examples of certain of these literary manifestations. Robert Burns, John Milton, Samuel Coleridge, and Francis Bacon also occasionally found ways to draw on the psalms. More recently, American poets who have reached back to those ancient poems for their own purposes include Daniel Berrigan, Robert Pinsky, Kathleen Norris, William Stafford, and Anthony Hecht. In fact, a psalm, such as 137, resembles the combination of brevity, situational setting, and thematic conveyance of many current postmodern American and English poems. The psalms often lend themselves to the contemporaneous and spontaneous, to the commonplace; as the American poet and writer Kathleen Norris has expressed the concept, ". . . the Psalms are blessedly untidy."[3] Or, as the martyr, renowned twentieth-century theologian, and sometime-poet Dietrich Bonhoeffer voiced, they "mirror life with all its ups and downs, its passions, and discouragements."[4]

The psalms have even helped allay literary feuds. For instance, in the 1950s both T. S. Eliot and C. S. Lewis, titans in the world of letters who disagreed on a great variety of subjects, were asked by the Church of England to serve on the Psalter Revision Commission for the retranslation of the psalms. Yet once Eliot and Lewis began to work on the psalms, the previously held antagonisms started to evaporate. According to writer Roger Kojecky:

> Their first meeting started inauspiciously with Eliot telling Lewis, ten years his junior, that he looked older than [he] appeared in his photos. Lewis had for years disliked Eliot's poetry and criticism ("a very great evil" he called it in a 1935

---

3. Kathleen Norris, *The Psalms* (New York: Riverhead Books, 1997), viii.
4. Dietrich Bonhoeffer, *Prayer Book of the Bible* (Minneapolis: Fortress Press, 2005), 147. Courtesy of Augsburg Fortress Publishers.

letter to Paul Elmer More), but somehow in the context of Psalter Revision Eliot must have won him over, since Lewis wrote afterwards that seeing him, he "loved him." In their exchanges of letters "Dear Mr Eliot" became "My dear Eliot."[5]

The ancient poems had broken through the borders of two well-organized and well-fortified states, or, as awakened by the words of Psalm 147, they could have said to each other they now saw "peace on your borders."[6]

Why do the psalms fascinate poets of every age? It may be as simple as the words of one poet who said a few years ago, meaning to be only half-facetious: "Poetry hasn't improved much since the psalms." Professor J. R. R. Tolkien of *The Hobbit* fame viewed the powers of oral tradition and poetry so favorably that he seemed to suggest in his work that the worst thing ever to happen to poetry was the printing press. One can infer from this attitude that poetry in the oral tradition, in which the psalms were initially enjoyed, had to be, by their very nature, like a conversation: immediate, attractive, intense, emotional, and very personal. Or, as similarly related through the words of Psalm 48, "As we have heard, so have we seen."[7]

---

5. Roger Kojecky, book review article: Barry Spurr, 'Anglo-Catholic in Religion': T. S. Eliot and Christianity, *The Glass*, Number 23, Spring 2011.

6. The Book of Common Prayer (New York: The Church Hymnal Corporation, 1979), 805.

7. Ibid., 651.

CHAPTER 5

∽

The Crucibles

I N THE SPRING OF 2015, my wife Freda and I traveled to London for a short stopover on our way to the Baltics. Soon after our arrival in London, I thought it a good idea for us to visit Lambeth Palace, location of the scriptorium, where Thomas Cranmer reputedly compiled the very first Book of Common Prayer, published in 1549. The Palace has also been, for centuries, the London residence of the Archbishop of Canterbury, head of the Church of England and, more recently, also head (first among equals) of the loosely constituted worldwide Anglican Communion. Of course, I should have considered making necessary arrangements with Lambeth in advance of our trip, but the immediate had displaced the important, as so often happens, for the several weeks prior to our leaving New York City. I discovered that all public tours of the Palace for the time we had scheduled to spend in London were fully booked. Not to be totally dissuaded, I sent out an e-mail blindly to addresses I secured on the Palace's website and described my particular interest in visiting Lambeth, stressing my previous involvement several decades earlier in helping to shape the text as it now appears in the Psalter for the 1979 Episcopal Book of Common Prayer. I had little expectation of any accommodating response, but to my delight and relief, I received an afternoon phone call a couple of days following my e-mail and was asked if Freda and I could come immediately to the Palace for a private tour; we had to leave without hesitation—no changing into more proper clothes, no comb through the hair, just rough and ready. So, off to Lambeth

Palace we scurried in a taxi, hardly knowing the directions, and with any propriety now no doubt flapping in the breeze, we tore over the Thames and through the snarled and snarling London streets. A charming, bright, and knowledgeable woman who had worked for years at Lambeth greeted us as soon as we cleared gate security and led us on a private walk back through centuries of English ecclesiastical and secular history—Lambeth, a place apparently referenced as far back as the Domesday Book in 1086 as part of the land survey of England, ordered by William the Conqueror.[1] Unabashedly, we marched our way through the time when the first church, a small one, had been built around 1200 as a compromise agreed to by the monks at Canterbury, who feared their significance would be compromised with a larger structure at Lambeth[2]; when Lambeth became a principal center for the English Reformation of the sixteenth century; when Reginald Pole, Archbishop for Mary I (better known as "Bloody Mary"), strove, for a brief period in the 1550s, to restore the dominion of the Roman Catholic Church; when Queen Elizabeth I's first Archbishop, Matthew Parker (known to generations as "Nosy Parker"), balanced the Catholic and Protestant factions of the Church of England and helped confirm and perpetuate the Reformation in England; and when Lambeth Palace incurred severe damage from incendiary bombs dropped during World War II.[3] But it was, in truth, for that singular figure, Thomas Cranmer, we had come to Lambeth Palace: the man, appointed at the age of forty-four by Henry VIII as Archbishop of Canterbury, who served in that role for twenty-three years from 1533–1556 during one of the most important periods in English history, who assisted in Henry VIII's divorce from Catherine of Aragon, and

1. Amanda J. Thomas, *The Lambeth Cholera Outbreak of 1848–1849: The Setting, Causes, Course and Aftermath of an Epidemic in London* (Jefferson, NC: McFarland & Co., 2010), 81.
2. Survey of London, Volume 23, Lambeth: South Bank and Vauxhall, Lambeth Palace, Chapter 22, London County Council, London, England, 1951.
3. George Bell, Chichester Diocesan Leaflet, October 1939, Lambeth Palace Library, Bell Papers, 72.

officiated at Henry's subsequent marriage to Anne Boleyn whom Cranmer had served as chaplain. Later, as Archbishop, Cranmer produced two English prayer books during the reign of Edward VI, one in 1549 and the other in 1552, that together established the precedent for future versions—including notably the 1662 edition—of the Book of Common Prayer, the principal model for worship among Anglicans and derivative branches of the Anglican Church throughout the world for more than three hundred years—the text that became the grand antecedent for the Book of Common Prayer of the Episcopal Church in the United States.

We were allowed to spend time in the Cranmer room, which is now part of the personal quarters for the Archbishop of Canterbury, with the restriction that one is not allowed to distribute photographs taken of the room. In the official guide to the Palace, the significance of the chamber is described as follows:

> . . . the room in the brick tower built in Cranmer's time where he is reputed to have worked and studied and prayed. It has been restored to commemorate his writing of the two Prayer Books of 1549 and 1552, which were consolidated to produce the Book of Common Prayer in 1662. This remained the only authorized service book providing forms of worship until 1980, and is a lasting memorial to Cranmer's scholarship and spirituality. His graceful prose still permeates the English language.[4]

The acid tests for revision to the Book of Common Prayer are, as ingeniously, rhetorically, and often stridently explained by W. H. Auden, the legacies of Thomas Cranmer and also of Miles Coverdale, who will be discussed later in this chapter. No institutional body could possibly contemplate any adjustments to the prayer book without weighing the deep-seated and intuitive loyalty that has existed and continues to exist among readers of and adherents to the Book of Common Prayer for these two sixteenth-century writers, and therein lies the relevance of these

---

4. Official Guide, Lambeth Palace, 32.

two "Crucibles." Auden understood this well and promoted the comparison between the work of these two writers and recent versions.

Nevertheless, while writing this book, I happened at one point to be reading a compilation of a few Cranmer collects. On the very first page of the first collect, the editor—a well-known, current writer in his own right—felt the need to explain the meaning (with several words constituting a parenthetical phrase for that purpose) of a rather archaic word, which Cranmer had utilized for a particular prayer book collect. This moment confirmed again the reason I had suspected for many years that neither "original" Cranmer nor "original" Coverdale would work in the sanctuaries of most churches today. Good, if not superb, though ancient, writing, of course, serves the needs of some, but clearly not all, especially those who know more about Facebook than they do about the Book of Common Prayer. Any words that require further explanation simply add one more opaque layer through which language must travel to penetrate the hearts and minds of those searching and seeking profundity beyond their own uncertainties.

In a most basic sense, I've concluded that Cranmer and Coverdale can take care of themselves; they have a following of loyal readers who compare their Elizabethan phrases to those of Shakespeare and other eminent writers. Indeed, these two spiritual writers have engineered the grouping of words in ways that will never be forgotten, anymore than Shakespeare's words. Cranmer and Coverdale's phraseology will continue as part of Western literary and spiritual culture for as long as that culture exists. Yes, Cranmer and Coverdale can take care of themselves. Four hundred years to inculcate the streams of abiding language and emotional elevation supply a good insurance policy for not being forgotten. Not insignificantly, both Thomas Cranmer and Miles Coverdale have Elizabeth I's longevity and her receptiveness to the Book of Common Prayer to thank for the infusion of their words into English idiom and style. As we explore the contributions of both Cranmer and Coverdale through the following pages, it would be wise to acknowledge the plenitude of phrases and rhetorical concepts that have been integrated into our language and into the various ways by which we often cope with modern and postmodern culture. We hardly notice the many uses to which the psalms in language and thought are applied to our everyday lives.

One appreciates Auden's loyalty to Cranmer (after all, Auden's most vociferous and severe complaints about revisions to the Book of Common Prayer dealt with adjustments to Cranmer's language), whose work was carried forward into subsequent prayer books, especially when observed from a viewpoint of the two primary effects that Cranmer's literature had on the future of English. First, there are the lines and phrases imprinted on our written and spoken words that epitomize parts of our English language. Second, when one examines the various poetic and literary devices employed in the 1549 Book of Common Prayer, it becomes clear that Cranmer was a master of many structural applications that were to become models during the Elizabethan period and well afterwards, including techniques suited for even today's writers.

An abundance of memorable phrases from Cranmer's Book of Common Prayer is guaranteed immortality within the English language. Just to mention a few examples: the following underlined words should be well-known iconic literature for English usage. With one notable exception, for which the 1552 version is summoned, the selections below are drawn from Cranmer's 1549 Book of Common Prayer. For purposes of historical clarification, Cranmer did not actually include the Psalter within his prayer books, but he did offer instructions on the manner in which the psalms should be utilized in connection with the contents of those prayer books. The Psalter was not formally part of the Book of Common Prayer until 1662.[5]

---

5. Brian Cummings, ed., *The Book of Common Prayer: The Texts of 1549, 1559, and 1662* (Oxford: Oxford University Press, 2011), lv.

From "*The Forme of Solemnizacion of Matrimonie*" (1549):

> to have and to holde from this day forwarde, for better, for wurse, for richer, for poorer, in sickenes, and in health, to love and to cherishe . . .

From "*The Ordre for the Buriall of the Dead*" (1549):

> I commende thy soule to God the father almighty, and thy body to the grounde, earth to earth, asshes to asshes, dust to dust, in sure and certayne hope of resurreccion to eternal life . . .

From "*The Administracion of Publyck Baptisme*" (1549):

> Minister. Doest thou forsake the devill and all his workes?
> Aunswere. I forsake them.
> Minister. Doest thou forsake the vaine pompe, and glory of the worlde, with all the covetouse desyres of the same?
> Aunswere. I forsake them.
> Minister. Doest thou forsake the carnall desyres of the flesh, so that thou wilt not folowe, nor be ledde by them?
> Aunswere. I forsake them.

Cranmer also authored for the Book of Common Prayer many other short phrases that consciously and subconsciously rise, in quick order, to our tongues when the occasion suits, such as "moveable feast," "peace in our time," "body and soul," "hardness of heart," and "in heart and mind," among many more. In fact, phrases contained in the Book of Common Prayer often rose to be iconic within our oral history, both public and private. According to Winfield Bevins, author of *Our Common Prayer*, "The words of the Prayer Book have become a familiar part of the English language, and after the Bible, it is the most frequently cited book in the *Oxford Dictionary of Quotations*."[6]

---

6. Winfield Bevins, *Our Common Prayer* (Simeon Press, 2015), 24.

Though not to diminish the literary acumen and accomplishments of Cranmer in the least, it is still relevant to acknowledge he benefited from several aids that supported him constantly during the drafting of the prayer book; even some of his best lines did not spring whole cloth from his own creation. For instance, the enduring lines of "earth to earth, ashes to ashes, dust to dust" actually represent a literal translation from the underlying Latin, "*terram terrae: cinerem cineri; pulverum pulveri.*" In addition, the infinitive phrase, "to love her and keep her in sickness and in health," drew from a York manual he relied upon as a resource that carried the phrase, "love her and kepe her in syknes and in helthe."[7]

Thomas Cranmer certainly enjoyed assistance in the composition of his books of common prayer, and it is especially unfortunate that no annotated edition of the sources—personal, liturgical, theological—exists, detailing the contributors and contributed works that made their way into Cranmer's text. We do know he relied on persons and texts from outside England, principally with German connections (including the words of Andreas Osiander, uncle to Cranmer's wife). Even Eastern Orthodox and Spanish liturgical influences found a path into his compilations. Furthermore, the work of homegrown translators and writers such as Richard Taverner and Cranmer's own staff members had their parts to play in the resultant phrasing. It is obvious that refined theology carried a significant role in the language manifested in the Cranmer work, and many different voices, both alive with and friendly to Cranmer and former ones, such as Augustine of Hippo and Paul, helped to direct his steps down the doctrinal path he led, shepherd of the English flock. Notwithstanding the conscious and subconscious influences that brought the prayer books to life, Diarmaid MacCulloch, in his wonderfully comprehensive and sensible biography, *Thomas Cranmer*, correctly gives to Cranmer his due praise: "Whatever help . . . Cranmer received, he should take credit for the overall job of editorship and the overarching structure

7. Cummings, *The Book of Common Prayer: The Texts of 1549, 1559, and 1662*, xvi.

of the book."[8] It would indeed be unfair to leave the impression that Cranmer's job was the clipping and pasting of others' compositions, for sufficient evidence exists to show that Cranmer's fine, original hand was at work in numerous spots throughout the volume, including his many collects. In places where he may not have produced the original piece, his alterations, extensions, and elaborations emphatically improved the final results.

The other remarkable aspect of Cranmer's memorable achievements is the variety of literary devices with which he paints the text. It is surely worth taking the time to examine the range of applications that Cranmer so effortlessly demonstrates—with effects that can impress the most scrupulous of readers. As I began to chart these devices in some organized fashion, it occurred to me that though we'll never know the extent to which subsequent Elizabethan writers owed a part of their own craft to lines learned from Cranmer's literary blueprints, there is no question that considerable influence was exerted over generations of notable English and American writers, including especially the Elizabethans, by Cranmer's two books of common prayer. For example, there are many samples in which Shakespeare's writings echo literary devices appearing in Cranmer. We also find them in other Elizabethan writers, such as John Donne, and in the Sidneys (Mary and Phillip), whose lyrical translation of the psalms secured their own place in literary history. Though technically not an Elizabethan, John Milton relied on techniques we see more than adequately employed by Cranmer. This effect on poets and writers who have gained enduring qualities should not be surprising since distribution measures were greatly expanded at the time of Cranmer's compilation, such as the act of Parliament that made the volume mandatory throughout England. There was an additional sweetener that even further encouraged maximum usage of the book—a royal decree by King Edward VI that set a ceiling

---

8. Diarmaid MacCulloch, *Thomas Cranmer* (New Haven and London: Yale University Press, 1996), 417.

on the price that could be charged for individual prayer books: "three shillings eightpence bound, or two shillings twopence for the leaves alone, for those who wished to have the book bound according to their particular preferences."[9] It would therefore not be too much of a reach to declare Thomas Cranmer the likely father of Elizabethan English.

While there may be more than one extant Cranmer illustration for each enlisted literary technique examined below and in Appendix I: Additional Examples of Literary Devices Employed by Thomas Cranmer in the Book of Common Prayer, I decided it could be a little laborious, if not boring, for readers (and for the author as well) to work their way through repeated cases offering the same point.

Anadiplosis: Repetition of a prominent word or phrase ending one clause to become the beginning of the subsequent clause.

Of the Administracion of publyke Baptisme (1549):

Priest with Others: I believe in God the father almightie.

Priest: Almightie and everlastyng God, heavenly father, we geve thee humble thankes . . .

Anaphora: Initial words for one clause or phrase repeated at the beginning of successive clauses or phrases.

An Ordre for Morninge Prayer; A generall confession (1552):

Almightie and moste mercifull father, *we have* erred and strayed from thy wayes, lyke loste shepe. *We have* folowed to much the devises and desyres of oure owne heartes. *We have* offended against thy holy lawes. *We have* left undone those thinges which we oughte to have done, and *we have* done those thyngs which we ought not to have done: and there is no health in us.

---

9. Alan Jacobs, *The Book of Common Prayer: A Biography* (Princeton, NJ: Princeton University Press, 2013), 65.

Metaphor: Use of a dissimilar object or concept in place of another word, creating a relationship that otherwise does not normally exist.

> The Supper of the Lorde, and the holy Communion, commonly called the Masse (1549):

> . . . we eate and drinke our owne damnacion . . .

To read poetry or fiction, one does not, as a rule, need to agree with the writer's religion, ethics, or politics, though it more often helps. I must admit I do not always think about some of William Faulkner's less known and less sympathetic comments about race while I read his fiction. Similarly, I do not constantly focus on T. S. Eliot's anti-Semitic lines as I read his verse, although I'm probably more inclined to recall Pound's pro-fascism attitudes expressed during World War II. It may just be I read Pound less often, which can cause me to be less familiar with his work, so that the public image rises more immediately to recognition than it otherwise would. Of course, each of these three writers is, for the most part, well respected within the literary community for his art (or attitude toward art), notwithstanding the shortcomings to which I've alluded. For our present purposes, we are more interested in the writing skills of Thomas Cranmer, as exhibited in his books of common prayer, than we are in his theological views. But judged fully, those views gave venue to the substance of his words; one plainly cannot divorce the consequential impact of Reformational convictions that inspired him from the words that ultimately made themselves the monumental essence of the 1549 and 1552 books of common prayer he compiled. Thus, may we call his language of poetry or prose, gathered so closely to a systematic theology to which he had become so individually bound, reflected in his books of common prayer, a form of art in the way we apply the appellation of artist to Faulkner, Eliot, or Pound? Only if we have the most narrow view can we not call his words art, as we have more than a few good reasons to name Thomas Cranmer the likely father of Elizabethan English.

One of the more fascinating and intriguing parts of diving into the sixteenth century—mainly, the first half of the sixteenth century—is the panoply of personages who would shape religious denominations, practices, and determinative theology in Reformational Protestantism for the next several hundred years: John Calvin, Thomas Cranmer, Martin Luther, John Knox, among many more. And almost as enticing is the way in which these phenomena often crossed paths with respect to theological and liturgical issues then facing the Church of England, such as the controversy between Cranmer and Knox over kneeling versus standing for communion, and communications to and by Luther and Calvin on matters being decided within England that were assumed to have far-reaching implications for the Reformational Protestant movement. Moreover, Erasmus, who, though a reformer, remained a Catholic for the entirety of his life, taught at Cambridge University during a time Cranmer was also there. According to Ashley Null in *Thomas Cranmer's Doctrine of Repentance*, Erasmus, through his humanist approach toward biblical text, certainly influenced Cranmer's views toward the scriptures.[10]

The history of the English arm of the Protestant Reformation, including the creation and practices of the Anglican Church and the related literary expressions given voice through Thomas Cranmer's prose and Coverdale's retranslated psalms, had weighty effects on W. H. Auden. Beyond the fact both of his grandfathers were members of the Anglican clergy, he referred with fondness to his time as a choirboy at a Church of England parish: "I had acquired a certain sensitivity to language which I could not have acquired in any other way."[11] I take that comment to be a whopping compliment for both Cranmer and Miles Coverdale. I've even wondered whether Auden's unapologetic proclivity later in life for routinely wearing slippers in public had its beginnings, at least in

---

10. Ashley Null, *Thomas Cranmer's Doctrine of Repentance* (Oxford: Oxford University Press, 2006), 86.

11. W. H. Auden, *A Certain World* (New York: The Viking Press, 1974), 73.

part (notwithstanding his somewhat famed foot problems), in the Anglo-Catholic practice by thurifers and other liturgical attendants of wearing slippers while performing duties during worship services.

W. H. Auden's admiration for Cranmer was obvious and sincere, demonstrable in his sentiments mentioning Cranmer's English alongside Shakespeare's. Regardless, I've come to realize that some of Auden's views would not have comported well with at least a couple of important attitudes carried by the former Archbishop. For example, in the July 6, 1971 letter to me, Auden describes his preferred idea for reform toward the Book of Common Prayer:

> [W]hat we should have done is the exact opposite of the Roman Catholics: we should have said, "Henceforth, we will have the Book of Common Prayer in Latin." (There happens to be an excellent translation.)[12]

To project Auden's presence in England at the time the 1549 Book of Common Prayer had been distributed to local parishes and his promotion of Latin instead of the vernacular for use in the prayer book, one can quite easily envision Auden being burned at the stake with Archbishop Cranmer himself eagerly stoking the flames. To Cranmer, a vernacular book of worship or Bible in English constituted a direct counterposition to the practice within the Roman church of employing Latin for religious texts and services. He saw Latin as a constant obstacle and obdurate impediment between the word of God and the individual in the pews of English churches. Several years after his appointment as Archbishop of Canterbury, Cranmer authorized for England a vernacular Bible, the Great Bible, as translated by Miles Coverdale. Cranmer mandated that each church parish in the realm have a copy of the Great Bible for its own, available for services and for members of the congregation. The Bible was normally chained somewhere in each church so that

---

12. Letter to J. Chester Johnson from W. H. Auden, dated July 6, 1971.

it could not be absconded with by overly zealous and devout readers. Since most worshipers in England at that point were illiterate, they would simply be able to see the Great Bible and witness its presence, although "priests were required to read the biblical passages appointed for any given service in Coverdale's English."[13]

This approach in developing a vernacular Bible for the masses followed in the wake of the work of that numinous Reformationist, Martin Luther, whose German vernacular translation, relying more on Greek than on Latin as an underlying text, preceded Coverdale's Great Bible. It is said that Luther, while working on his German Bible, made trips to places where people were gathered in order to hear speech that could help him translate the words of the Bible into a more contemporary German language. Because Miles Coverdale completed much of his retranslation work for the English vernacular Bible on the continent while in exile, he had less opportunity for his English version to follow a similar practice.

The whole exercise of compiling and producing a prayer book was meant to be a way of removing barriers that separated the clergy from their people and God from God's people, of removing a secret spiritual message known by only a few and communicated in a distant and impervious language, Latin. For Cranmer, a vernacular Bible and prayer book democratized the road to God's kingdom, and the approach he took, in this respect, formed one of the enduring pillars for the Reformational foundation he wished to build and mold appositely for England.

In the same 1971 letter, Auden describes his perception of the meaning of communion—the Mass, the Eucharist, the Rite—which, to him, was a mystical experience that brought the past and future together. According to Auden, "[T]he Rite—preaching, of course, is another matter—is the link between the dead and the unborn. This calls for a timeless language which, in practice, means a dead language."[14] In the same way that the contrast

---

13. Jacobs, *The Book of Common Prayer: A Biography*, 13.
14. Letter to J. Chester Johnson from W. H. Auden, dated July 6, 1971.

between Auden's and Cranmer's respective ideas about Latin as the language venue for worship couldn't have been starker, their contrary viewpoints toward the purposes, practices, and passions of the Eucharist also could hardly have been more different. Rather than communion being a turn toward the past to accommodate the dead, as suggested by Auden, the Rite was, to Cranmer, strictly for the living: those who were physically present and actually partaking in the celebration and ceremony at that particular point in time. MacCulloch has also written astutely about the attitude of the evangelists, of which Cranmer was demonstrably and surely one, for the Reformation and related liturgical conduct toward the Mass, the communion, the Eucharist:

> For the late medieval Church, the mass had become as much something for the dead as for the living; it had broken down the barrier between life and death in a very particular, concrete sense. Behind the crowds of the faithful in a medieval parish church, convent church or cathedral jostled invisible crowds, the crowds of the dead. And they crowded in because the Church maintained a model of the afterlife in which the mass could speed the souls of the faithful departed through purgatory. . . . It was to change this that the reformers struggled. Insisting that the just shall live by faith alone, they believed that the medieval Church, with the papacy as its evil genius, had played a gigantic confidence trick on the living by claiming to aid the dead in this way. They sought to banish the dead, and to banish the theology which had summoned them into the circle of the living faithful gathered round the Lord's table.[15]

The reformers in the sixteenth century were less preoccupied with "the unborn" in the Eucharist than they were with eliminating, as they saw it, the dead's unjustified and consequential role at communion, and it is quite reasonable to conclude that Cranmer would have found Auden's proposition not only unacceptable but,

---

15. MacCulloch, *Thomas Cranmer*, 613–14.

more likely, even impalpable. Not surprisingly, as evidence of Cranmer's strong feelings about changing the focus of the event at "the Lord's table," he began to disassociate the moment from papacy practices by downplaying the term "mass," though it remained a term in the 1549 Book of Common Prayer. The term was less favorable to him than "The Supper of the Lorde, and the holy Communion." Cranmer completely eliminates the term "mass" in his 1552 Book of Common Prayer, referring to the event as "The order for the administration of the Lordes Supper or holye Communion." Period. No mention of the mass, no invoking of a journey for the dead, no invasion from the papacy.

The bread and wine within a Eucharist retained their physical natures and were not transformed into the body and blood of Christ, for no transubstantiation existed. Rather, the body and blood of Christ came to the receiver of the bread and wine not physically, but spiritually, with the bread and wine simply representing Christ crucified to Cranmer. There was no adoration of the Eucharistic elements; there would be no concrete altar, but an ordinary table for the Lord's Supper. Kneeling was allowed, but the gesture meant no adoration for the bread and wine, as the "Black Rubric" had specifically instructed in the addendum to his 1552 Book of Common Prayer. Though Cranmer did not believe an addendum in the form of the "Black Rubric" had been necessary, he composed the language to mollify concerns of more radical reformers, including John Knox, who preferred for the communion to be taken while standing, which meant an even more informal and personal participation in the Lord's Supper around the Lord's table. Cranmer traversed a rather narrow track between those who maintained an allegiance to the papist forms of worship and those radical reformers we may assign to the Anabaptist camp, but in the cases for a vernacular Bible and the Eucharist being strictly an event for the living participants, his partiality for the Reformationists' convictions was translucent.

The more I've learned about Cranmer, the more I've come to the conclusion that his responsibility in the writing and compiling of the 1549 and 1552 prayer books was only one of many realm-shaping challenges with which he had to deal during the time he occupied the position of Archbishop of Canterbury, a period extending for twenty-three years until he was executed at Oxford by auto-da-fé, death for heresy by being burned at the stake. Flesh and sinew furnished fuel for the fires of the executed. The killing of Cranmer had been called for by Mary I, the Catholic monarch who followed the reign of young Edward VI (born 1537; died 1553). Proxy leaders in England ruled on behalf of Edward for much of his kingship, when the Protestant Reformation in England flourished, including the widespread use of Cranmer's prayer books.

Well before Cranmer became Archbishop, he had worked earnestly on Henry VIII's divorce from Catherine of Aragon, and Cranmer's consecration to his new position fell less than two months before he declared Henry's divorce from Catherine final on May 23, 1533. During Cranmer's archbishopric, England underwent monumental changes. It was no small matter during the first part of his tenure for Cranmer, along with Henry VIII's chief advisor, Thomas Cromwell, to have responsibility for the development of the institutional framework and infrastructure for the entirely new entity, the Church of England, of which Cranmer's books of common prayer would be a part. Not insignificantly, there was the issue of church property: the method and means of seizure of property—whose, where, and how much? By expropriation of church properties with Cranmer as Archbishop, huge amounts of church land and buildings came under the jurisdiction of the Crown and, in turn, the Church of England. Then, what about the tenets, practices, and canon law to keep the clergy and faithful in line for this new Church of England in the face of a continuation of Catholicism's unrelenting course to remain the preeminent religion in the country? If the new church were to attain relevance for a populace steeped in centuries of Catholicism, it could not stray too far from the previous teachings. The country had moved, in concert with so many other Christians on the continent, away from Catholicism

toward evangelical Reformation (notwithstanding the fact that
Henry VIII, during his reign, still relied on many essential parts
of Catholic practices and beliefs, such as transubstantiation), and
the Church of England would have to adhere to, if not lead, this
tidal wave of awakening. Yet, England would need to go along its
own path, led by the Archbishop himself, who would address, by
authoring tracts, preaching sermons, writing letters, conducting
personal persuasions, and seeking (though not achieving) consensus for the pivotal theological and related issues of the age, such
as: soteriology, justification, popery and princes, the nexus of faith
and good works, predestination, confession, celibacy and marriage
of clergy, penance, and more. Then there were the investigations
of possible heresies and any work to be done arising from secular
governance relating to Cranmer's spheres of authority or attitude;
and, of course, the great time-eater and attention-consumer of politics: the necessity of staying in the good graces of sovereigns or their
ruling proxies. When and how could the Book of Common Prayer
be written and compiled with all of those other obligations claim-
ing time and focus? England demanded its own popular version—it
must and would be realized.

We now move on to that second pillar, Miles Coverdale, who,
along with Cranmer, held the Book of Common Prayer above any
threat of a serious revision for over four hundred years. Cranmer
and Coverdale were alike in one critical way, but quite different in
others. They had both become serious Reformationists early and
remained so for the rest of their lives. There is considerable evidence that Coverdale's views toward reform grew even stronger as
he aged, as exemplified by his resignation and departure from a
final cleric position over the religious garb he would be expected
to wear under an injunction issued by Queen Elizabeth I. Coverdale opposed any intimations of grand attire that rose to simili-
tude with the Catholic dress for priests. While both Coverdale and
Cranmer dedicated themselves to the vernacular, whether by prayer
book or Bible, as a key element of their respective Reformational
agendas, the relationship each had with John Knox, the Protestant

Reformationist and acknowledged founder of the Presbyterian Church in Scotland who adhered to deep Puritan strands, illustrates the comparative attitudes taken by Cranmer and Coverdale in matters of the movement. For example, Knox exerted so much pressure on Cranmer to remove kneeling from communion that Cranmer grudgingly accepted an addendum, the "Black Rubric," for the 1552 prayer book. It is clear Cranmer considered Knox a member of the more radical Puritan elements of the reform movement. Knox and Coverdale, on the other hand, were so comfortably in sync that six years after the "Black Rubric" was appended to the 1552 Book of Common Prayer, Coverdale agreed to be godfather to Knox's son at a service in Geneva, Switzerland, when the two were in exile on the continent.[16] It is therefore not surprising that Miles Coverdale, on the Reformationist scale, would have been seen as at least a tinge more radical than Thomas Cranmer.

In terms of other differences, Cranmer demonstrated a tolerance and survival for high political and administrative position and intrigue, notwithstanding his dramatic martyr's death at the end, an auto-da-fé that Coverdale was able to escape. Cranmer prevailed and excelled for much of his tenure as Archbishop of Canterbury during a most turbulent and consequential period of English history. On the other hand, Coverdale, who has been, on occasion, characterized by knowledgeable sources as an artist, steered a more narrow course, resting almost solely on the translated word, especially as directed toward an English-language Bible. From 1551–1553, Coverdale did serve as bishop of Exeter—the highest administrative position of his life—but he quickly departed and apparently never again harbored any desire to serve in a lofty bishopric role. There are facts that suggest he even shunned or deflected those possible opportunities. Even though he did serve in cleric positions for various parishes and in tutorial and lower-level educational roles, the most responsible administrative role he

---

16. J. F. Mozley, *Coverdale and His Bibles* (Cambridge: James Clarke & Co., 2005), 22. Courtesy of James Clarke & Co.

sought was that of managing the translation of large tracts of text and associated publication matters. Coverdale obviously felt more comfortable in confronting a body of untranslated biblical material than he did in confronting a body of unled Christians.

Miles Coverdale lived out his life in pursuit of the one salient goal of producing an elusive—at least in the form he desired—vernacular biblical scripture in English, an ambition that grew from the inspiration, evidenced in the excerpt from a letter he wrote to Thomas Cromwell, probably in 1527, before Coverdale had reached his fortieth birthday. Coverdale had been in the eye of Cromwell and Thomas More for several years, both of whom recognized his special talents. Later, the relationship with Cromwell proved particularly beneficial with respect to the Great Bible project that resided under Cromwell's aegis.

> Now I begin to taste of holy scriptures; now, honour be to God, I am set to the most sweet smell of holy letters, with the godly savour of holy and ancient doctors, unto whose knowledge I cannot attain without diversity of books, as is not unknown to your most excellent wisdom. Nothing in the world I desire but books as concerning my learning. They once had, I do not doubt but almighty God shall perform that in me which he, of his most plentiful favour and grace, hath begun.[17]

The mission Coverdale chose proved a quite difficult one. He departed England three times in exile, surviving a perilous change in monarchs and in the face of threats mainly from those conservatives in England who opposed the Reformationists. Exile became such a common occurrence for so many English during this period that Coverdale and fellow English Reformationists apparently had a code word for the exile, "Egypt," referring back in time to the departure by many Jews from Jerusalem and Judea to Egypt in order to escape impending slavery, forced diaspora, imprisonment,

---

17. W. S. Peterson, Introduction to *Psalms: The Coverdale Translation*, www.synaxis.info/psalter/5_english/c_psalms/CoverdalePsalms.pdf, 2.

torture, or execution. On occasion, Coverdale's books were burned in England and on the continent for being heretical. To emphasize the danger he confronted, soon after Mary I's ascent to the throne, speculation ran high that Coverdale would certainly be one of the next burned at the stake as a heretic. Except for the intervention of the King of Denmark on Coverdale's behalf, which allowed him to leave England, the speculation of death by auto-da-fé would likely have come true.[18] Though it is not an exaggeration to say he died impoverished and somewhat obscure, Coverdale's life proved to be exceedingly productive and long. Indeed, he was past eighty on the day of his death in early 1569. He had even fallen victim a few years earlier to the plague but recovered.

The repetitive use of one portrait of Coverdale intimates its authenticity, but J. F. Mozley, author of *Coverdale and His Bibles*, states that the portrait frequently utilized for Coverdale was somehow inaccurately assigned to him; in truth, Coverdale died without one.[19] History has provided us with more than one portrait of Thomas Cranmer, but we can only imagine—with virtually no guidelines for the purpose—the likely appearance of the person whose legacy had such a profound effect on the formation of the Bible in English and on literature and liturgy for English-speaking peoples.

Even so, Miles Coverdale is one of those key figures of Western civilization that history could have forgotten or misplaced—like persons of his time who are now hardly remembered at all: Richard Taverner, George Joye, and Pagninus. We know Coverdale died in proximate obscurity, and yet, here is someone who produced one of the seminal translations into English of the Bible in 1535, relying, in part, on the earlier work of William Tyndale—the Bible also being embroidered with a title page that carried a woodcut border ascribed to a design by Hans Holbein the Younger.[20] Soon

---

18. Mozley, *Coverdale and His Bibles*, 20.
19. Ibid., 28.
20. Ibid., 68.

thereafter, Coverdale was chosen to produce the Great Bible, with churches in England being mandated to have a copy on the premises. However, we can legitimately ask why Coverdale was chosen for the Great Bible. Mozley offers the following explanation:

> That Coverdale should be chosen to edit the GREAT BIBLE was only to be expected. The book was Cromwell's enterprise, and Coverdale had long been friend and supporter to that statesman. But he was also the fittest man for the task, and we cannot doubt that Cranmer, if he was consulted, approved the choice. Coverdale had a longer and wider experience of bible-translation than any other Englishman . . . and his modesty, industry, conciliatory temper and readiness to learn from any quarter made it likely that he would produce a presentable piece of work and one not unsuited to the needs of the times.[21]

But it was Coverdale's psalms that have been his principal claim to fame, predominantly as a result of their association with the 1549 Book of Common Prayer and as emended in prayer books thereafter. It was to these psalms that W. H. Auden devoted a considerable defense by raising his considerable voice against a retranslation that could diminish the influence and poetry of Coverdale—the psalms that reflected, in the words of William S. Peterson, Coverdale's "superb ear, an extraordinary sense of English prose rhythms, and a fluency which skillfully blended disparate elements."[22]

The psalms have been called by Dietrich Bonhoeffer the prayer book of the Bible,[23] and the psalms of Coverdale's Bible were considered so singular, favored, and loved by the English people in the early part of the seventeenth century that the King James Bible made only "slight alterations" before including them in that majestic opus.[24] In the early 1660s, debate occurred over whether the

---

21. Ibid., 201.

22. Peterson, Introduction to *Psalms: The Coverdale Translation*, 3.

23. Bonhoeffer, *Prayerbook of the Bible*, 156.

24. Adam Nicolson, *God's Secretaries: The Making of the King James Bible* (New York: HarperCollins, 2004), 249.

then recent version of the psalms, as rendered in the King James translation, or the Miles Coverdale version of the psalms, which had been savored by and imprinted upon Anglicans from the first Book of Common Prayer, should be carried forward in the 1662 Book of Common Prayer. In truth, the Coverdale retranslation had achieved so much acceptance among the Anglicans that when the Anglican Church adopted the King James scriptures for the epistles and gospels, Coverdale's older retranslation of the Psalter was retained for the 1662 Book of Common Prayer, and Coverdale's rendition has been present ever since, subject to only minor adjustments—until recently.

Like Auden, Miles Coverdale had been born, according to the best sources available, in York (the year of Coverdale's birth is debatable, but 1488 is not a bad guesstimate) and, also like Auden, he had relatives who served in cleric positions. But unlike Auden, who exhibited certain High Church proclivities that were seemingly inherited from and shaped in part by his mother, Coverdale proved to be more puritan in his religious practices and preferences.[25] Also, unlike Auden, whose close relatives were trained in the scientific, medical, and professional fields, Coverdale's relatives apparently derived their livelihoods from more basic occupations. Yet, despite these differences and others, such as the dissimilar epochs that characterized their disparate life conditions, one can conceivably imagine a special commonality they shared in appreciation for the English language and its mellifluous styles, both written and spoken.

While all English-language prayer books of the Anglican tradition have included a Psalter based on a retranslation contained in the 1540 Great Bible by Miles Coverdale, his work, like that of Jerome, was not derived directly from the original Hebrew.[26] Coverdale apparently had facility in Latin, Greek, and German, but

---

25. Edward Mendelson, *Early Auden* (New York: The Viking Press, 1981), xxii.
26. Charles M. Guilbert, *The Prayer Book Psalter Revised* (New York: The Church Hymnal Corporation, 1973), V.

very little familiarity with Hebrew. As a result of his limitations with Hebrew, Coverdale, according to Professor S. L. Greenslade,

> . . . knew well enough that he could not excel as a pure scholar so that his choice between authorities was frequently not determined by erudition so much as by his sense of style.[27]

Therefore, notwithstanding Coverdale's exceptional sense of style, it has long been known that his version was materially flawed with inaccuracies. In 1898, the biblical scholar S. R. Driver stated,

> Coverdale, it is evident, must have been a natural master of English style, and must have possessed a natural aptitude for finding felicitous turns of expression, and for casting them into harmonious and finely-rolling periods. But the warmest admirers of Coverdale's work must allow that it is disfigured by many inaccuracies. . . .[28]

Auden acknowledged this shortcoming, reflected in his repeated references to the inaccuracies permeating Coverdale's Psalter.

In recognition of Coverdale's style for graceful and canorous lines, there is an apocryphal story about Coverdale, the Psalter, and Shakespeare that deserves mention here; this story is known to have been repeated over multiple generations. It goes like this: As Coverdale was retranslating the Psalter in the sixteenth century, he would visit a certain pub each night, the same pub that was then frequented by Shakespeare. So, whenever Coverdale ran into a problem rendering a difficult passage into English, he would simply ask Shakespeare his opinion over a glass of malt, wine, or whatever they were drinking at the time. In this story, Shakespeare was actually responsible for key parts of the translated Psalter in the Coverdale version. However, the dates don't work (Shakespeare was only four when Coverdale died) and the geography doesn't

---

27. S. L. Greenslade, Introduction to *The Coverdale Bible 1535* (Folkestone: Wm. Dawson & Sons, 1975), 48 plus unnumbered leaves.

28. S. R. Driver, ed., *The Parallel Psalter* (Oxford: Clarendon Press, 1898), xxiv.

work (Coverdale apparently did much of his work on the Psalter while he lived on the continent in exile). Thus, the story is only apocryphal, but it still has had its particular message over time: keep your hands off of Coverdale if you know what's good for the congregants of the Anglican/Episcopal Church.

The loyalty of W. H. Auden is only representative of the broad and deep constituency that exists throughout the English-speaking world for the Psalter of Miles Coverdale, as certain lines are honored by and embedded auricularly in English-speaking peoples. Since Coverdale had only limited knowledge of Hebrew and relied primarily on other translations or retranslations for his psalms, the more accurate term for his efforts and exercise would be retranslated, as opposed to translated, which implies a direct rendering from the original text.

There are considerable and recognizable differences in the styles applied by the two "Crucibles" to their words, reflecting the nature and purpose of the contents. Lines of Coverdale's psalms are more urgent, less cerebral and abstract, than much of Cranmer's; they are also more intimate, more specific, and more contextual. But after all, the psalms were composed as poems, and the intensity of engagement and passion in the poetry is markedly personal and evident with Coverdale. Obviously, one cannot credit him, as retranslator, with the tone or the message of the underlying psalms, though one can credit him with the English, and I believe that is what most of us have done, all who have admired and often memorized many of his fortunate and insistent lines.

Admittedly, I'm about to be highly subjective in the choices I have made for favored parts of Coverdale's psalms—parts, I believe, that have settled into the conscious and subconscious labyrinths of memory and selection that will continue to be instantly recallable—although I prefer to think I'm being somewhat democratic and responsive to the choices I've also heard from friends, mentors, and colleagues. The following Coverdale selections of the psalms are taken from the 1540 Great Bible and then adjusted further, as previously described. Any alterations he made to his original 1535 Psalter version had largely, by the printing of the 1540 Great Bible, been congealed into a fixed repertoire. According to Canon Guilbert, Coverdale had, between 1535 and 1540, the benefit of a work by Sebastian Münster of Heidelberg that was "an edition of the Hebrew Old Testament, accompanied by a new Latin translation of it. On the basis of this new Latin version, Coverdale largely revised his 1535 text of the Psalms."[29]

Whatever the cause, there is no doubt that Coverdale extensively edited his 1535 psalms, and by the 1540 Great Bible, he had essentially finished the retranslation that would establish his mark, resulting in the inclusion of his psalms in future editions of the prayer book. The word spellings and the punctuation for the excerpts from the psalms of the 1540 Great Bible set forth below have been adjusted to make them, while not fully modernized, more understandable to current readers.

Selections are separated into three groups. First, there are longer pieces, resembling quasi-stanzas, in which related sentiments and structures merge into units of several, successive lines taken directly from the individual psalms chosen. Second, single lines or single sentences that are especially recognizable from Coverdale's Psalter have been presented individually to emphasize their acknowledged sufficiency to stand alone in recollection. Third, our English language is sprinkled with numerous phrases that originally appeared in or were derived from the psalms of Coverdale, and this section offers a sampling of a few such constructions. Auden said, more than once, that the English language of the sixteenth century should be comprehensible for the twentieth-century reader. In a sense he is right, but the truth of his comment depends on the piece—that is, looking backward with a more modern text, one can, generally speaking, discern the meaning and intent of Coverdale's Psalter of 1540 without much adaptation. That being said, in the absence of such a crib, I think Auden's statement a little expansive.

---

29. Guilbert, *The Psalter: A New Version for Public Worship and Private Devotion*, x.

Set forth below is a representative sampling of the first group: longer excerpts from Coverdale's Psalter with poetic stanza characteristics.

Out of the mouth of very babes and sucklings
hast thou ordained strength because of thine enemies,
    that thou mightest still the enemy and the avenger.
For I will consider thy heavens, even the works of thy fingers,
    the moon and the stars, which thou hast ordained.
What is man that thou art mindful of him,
    and the son of man that thou visitest him?
Thou madest him lower than the angels
    to crown him with glory and worship.
Thou makest him to have dominion in the works of thy hands,
    and thou hast put all things in subjection under his feet.
    (Psalm 8:2–6)

The heavens declare the glory of God,
    and the firmament showeth his handiwork.
One day telleth another,
    and one night certifieth another.
There is neither speech nor language,
    but their voices are heard among them.
Their sound is gone out into all lands,
    and their words into the ends of the world.
In them hath he set a tabernacle for the sun,
    which cometh forth as a bridegroom out of his chamber
    and rejoiceth as a giant to run his course. (Psalm 19:1–5)

The Lord is my shepherd;
    therefore can I lack nothing.
He shall feed me in a green pasture
    and lead me forth beside the waters of comfort.
He shall convert my soul
    and bring me forth in the paths of righteousness for his Name's sake.
Yea, though I walk through the valley of the shadow of death,

I will fear no evil,
    for thou art with me;
    thy rod and thy staff comfort me.
Thou shalt prepare a table before me against them that trouble me;
    thou hast anointed my head with oil,
    and my cup shall be full.
But thy loving kindness and mercy shall follow me all the days of my life,
    and I will dwell in the house of the Lord for ever.
    (Psalm 23)

Thou shalt open my lips, O Lord;
    my mouth shall show thy praise.
For thou desirest no sacrifice, else would I give it thee;
    but thou delightest not in burnt-offerings.
The sacrifice of God is a troubled spirit;
    a broken and a contrite heart, O God, shalt thou not despise.
    (Psalm 51:15–17)

For the Lord is a great God,
    and a great King above all gods.
In his hand are all the corners of the earth,
    and the strength of the hills is his also.
The sea is his, and he made it;
    and his hands prepared the dry land.
O come, let us worship and fall down
    and kneel before the Lord our maker.
For he is the Lord, our God,
and we are the people of his pasture and the sheep of his hands.
    (Psalm 95:3–7)

O be joyful in the Lord, all ye lands;
    serve the Lord with gladness
    and come before his presence with a song.
Be ye sure that the Lord he is God;
it is he that hath made us, and not we ourselves;
    we are his people and the sheep of his pasture.

O go your way into his gates with thanksgiving,
and into his courts with praise;
>   be thankful unto him and speak good of his Name.
For the Lord is gracious;
his mercy is everlasting;
>   and his truth endureth from generation to generation. (Psalm 100)

I will lift up mine eyes unto the hills
>   from whence cometh my help.
My help cometh even from the Lord,
>   which hath made heaven and earth.
He will not suffer thy foot to be moved,
>   and he that keepeth thee will not sleep.
Behold, he that keepeth Israel
>   shall neither slumber nor sleep. (Psalm 121:1–4)

Except the Lord build the house,
>   their labour is but lost that build it.
Except the Lord keep the city,
>   the watchman waketh but in vain.
It is but lost labour that ye haste to rise up early and so late
take rest and eat the bread of carefulness;
>   for so he giveth his beloved sleep.
Lo, children and the fruit of the womb
>   are an heritage and gift
>   that cometh of the Lord. (Psalm 127:1–4)

By the waters of Babylon we sat down and wept,
>   when we remembered thee, O Sion.
As for our harps, we hanged them up,
>   upon the trees that are therein.
For they that led us away captive required of us then a song
and melody in our heaviness:
>   "Sing us one of the songs of Sion."
How shall we sing the Lord's song
>   in a strange land? (Psalm 137:1–4)

For lo, there is not a word in my tongue,
    but thou, O Lord, knowest it altogether.
Thou hast fashioned me behind and before
    and laid thine hand upon me.
Such knowledge is too wonderful and excellent for me;
    I cannot attain unto it.
Whither shall I go then from thy Spirit,
    or whither shall I go then from thy presence?
If I climb up into heaven, thou art there;
    if I go down to hell, thou art there also.
If I take the wings of the morning
    and remain in the uttermost parts of the sea,
Even there also shall thy hand lead me
    and thy right hand shall hold me. (Psalm 139:3–9)

Although they may not rise to a category such as a quasi-stanza, the following lines from Coverdale's Psalter illustrate the second grouping and are worthy of significant mention in light of the historical, literary, and spiritual heritage they have conveyed to us since the sixteenth century.

Let the words of my mouth and the meditation of my heart
be alway acceptable in thy sight,
    O Lord, my strength and my redeemer. (Psalm 19:14)

My God, my God, look upon me; why hast thou forsaken me?
    (Psalm 22:1)

Yea, though I walk through the valley of the shadow of death,
I will fear no evil,
    for thou art with me;
    thy rod and thy staff comfort me. (Psalm 23:4)

The Lord is my light and my salvation;
whom then shall I fear?
    The Lord is the strength of my life;
    of whom then shall I be afraid? (Psalm 27:1)

Thou shalt open my lips, O Lord;
  my mouth shall show thy praise. (Psalm 51:15)

For he considered that they were but flesh,
  and that they were even a wind that passeth away
  and cometh not again. (Psalm 78:40)

O teach us to number our days
  that we may apply our hearts unto wisdom. (Psalm 90:12)

O come, let us sing unto the Lord;
  let us heartily rejoice in the strength of our salvation. (Psalm 95:1)

The fear of the Lord is the beginning of wisdom. (Psalm 111:10)

Thy word is a lantern unto my feet
  and a light unto my paths. (Psalm 119:105)

Similar to Cranmer's writings, numerous memorable phrases in the English language have come or have been derived from Coverdale's psalms. To acknowledge only a few, consider: "gray-headed," "apple of an/my eye," "poor and needy," "tender mercy/mercies," "softer than butter," "heart's desire," "saving health," "put to shame," "strength to strength," "green/greener pastures," "green as the grass," "corners of the earth." Just, for example, the use of the phrase "greener pastures," which we frequently include in normal speech, harkens back to Psalm 23: "He shall feed me in a green pasture." Or the "distant" or "four" "corners of the earth"—again, going back to Coverdale in Psalm 95: "In his hand are all the corners of the earth." Of course, we poets and writers owe him a ton of gratitude for sprucing up and enriching our native tongue with phrases like these, which we have often stolen without the slightest hint of attribution or acknowledgment.

Like Cranmer, Coverdale demonstrated a special facility with literary devices that would leave their effects on much sixteenth-century and Elizabethan literature. Coverdale was at least Cranmer's equal in the effective application of favorable outcomes from these literary techniques. Following the approach enlisted previously for Cranmer, one sample by Coverdale for each literary device should be an adequate demonstration. Over and above those set forth below, Appendix II: Additional Examples of Literary Devices Employed by Miles Coverdale in the Psalms of the Great Bible of 1540 illustrates his capabilities.

> *Anadiplosis: Repetition of a prominent word or phrase that ends one clause to become the beginning of the subsequent clause.*
>
> I will lift up mine eyes unto the hills from whence cometh my help. My help cometh even from the Lord, which hath made heaven and earth. (Psalm 121:1–2)

> *Metaphor: Use of a dissimilar object or concept in place of another word, creating a relationship that otherwise does not normally exist.*
>
> . . . the dew of thy birth is of the womb of the morning. (Psalm 110:3b)

> *Parallelism: A clause or set of words within individual lines having a similar structure and related concepts to other immediately proximate lines.*
>
> They have mouth and speak not; eyes have they and see not. They have ears and hear not; noses have they and smell not. They have hands and handle not; feet have they and walk not . . . (Psalm 115:5–7a)

It is with no small regret we now leave "The Crucibles" as a primary focus. One must be more than a little infected and moved, if not motivated, by the gravitas of their lives and respective missions. There is an old saw that the epoch shapes its visionaries, but I heartily disagree—rather, the reverse is true. These two shaped their epoch: Cranmer, who died a martyr, even though he waffled terribly before the final act; and Coverdale, who would have likely accepted and known immolation himself, but for the vagaries of history. Few people are ever equipped to deal consequently with history, but imbued with rebellion, intelligence, and quickened discomfort at an inherited religion and disturbing spiritual voices, Cranmer and Coverdale forged a reformed faith, new concepts, new words, new rhythms, and a landscape for an anonymous future—a place where they continue, in many ways, to impact and define our own world still, nearly half a millennium later.

CHAPTER 6

❧

Auden in Print

N HIS EXCEPTIONALLY COMPREHENSIVE and illuminating book, *W. H. Auden: A Commentary*, John Fuller states that Auden had occasionally "modulated into psalmody" in his poetry.[1] Fuller explains this modulation consisted of "rhetorical balance with colon and semi-colon, linked repetitions, address to absolutes, sense of abasement and hope, etc., as at least a kind of free verse with a 17th century British model."[2] Even though Auden would voice his affection for and the poetic influence from the words of the Book of Common Prayer, including its psalmody, Miles Coverdale does not appear to be given attention in Auden's verse—and neither does Thomas Cranmer for that matter, though the theological and associated issues with which the two Reformationists often contended rise rather frequently in his poems. The concerns these two Reformationists confronted, such as the spiritual authority of the Pope and papacy and the ecclesiastical role of temporal governance by earthly "princes," manifested in Henry VIII, Edward VI, and Mary I, are often relevant subjects for Auden's poetry, with references to "Caesar" and the "Pope" (or equivalencies and metonymies) appearing in both short and long poems, including his dramas in verse. Of course, the rich interplay of church and state in English life, where separation of the two does not exist as it does in

---

1. John Fuller, *W. H. Auden: A Commentary* (Princeton, NJ: Princeton University Press, 1998), 251.
2. Email to J. Chester Johnson from John Fuller, dated August 27, 2016.

the United States, was likely to have been examined and vetted by Auden and his family, with both of his grandfathers being members of the Anglican clergy.

It is a bit surprising Auden hardly mentions Thomas Cranmer or Miles Coverdale in his writings, recognizing those strong beliefs, as he worked to retain their writings within the Book of Common Prayer. A notable exception to this generalization happens, quite coincidentally, in October 1967, only a few weeks before Auden returns from England to New York. Upon his arrival, he experienced a new trial Episcopal liturgy—apparently for the first time—at his neighborhood church, St. Mark's Church-in-the-Bowery, an event that results in his famous letter to the rector, Father J. C. Michael Allen, which characterized the new liturgy as "appalling." In his letter, dated November 20, 1967, which will be covered in more detail in a subsequent chapter, he ardently states, "I implore you by the bowels of Christ to stick to Cranmer and King James."[3]

The previous month, Auden had given the inaugural series of presentations for the commemorative T. S. Eliot lectures at the University of Kent in Canterbury and had chosen for Lecture One the subject, "The Martyr as Dramatic Hero," in which he discusses, in a rather wide-ranging manner, Charles Williams's play, *Thomas Cranmer of Canterbury*, with special emphasis on Cranmer as both protagonist and historical figure. These commemorative lectures would be published as a volume entitled *Secondary Worlds* the following year. From the very first time Auden raises Cranmer in any crucial way for the lecture, we know we will hear more decisive and active words about the former Archbishop of Canterbury: "He (Cranmer) was, that is to say, both a man of action and an artist, a maker."[4]

Later, Auden explains the danger posed for an artist—a man of words, if you will: words can become a form of idolatry for such a person who separates meaning from the delights of expression. It is

---

3. Letter to Father J. C. Michael Allen from W. H. Auden, dated November 20, 1967. Courtesy of the Archives of the Episcopal Church.
4. W. H. Auden, *Secondary Worlds* (New York: Random House, 1968), 24.

intriguing to contemplate whether Auden believed he himself had become subject to the same temptation (I think he realized that he had, but it wouldn't stop him from aggressively pursuing his own support of Cranmer and Coverdale, even if some of their expressions had lost currency and accurate meaning) to idolize words, a characteristic he applies to Cranmer in the lecture.

> Whatever or whomever we love carries with it a temptation to its own special kind of idolatry: those who, like Cranmer, love words, are tempted to idolize them; idolatry of the word can express itself, according to the temperament of the individual, either in a fanatic dogmatism which identifies language with truth, or in an aestheticism which sets beauty of language above truth. For Cranmer, essentially a timid and gentle man, it was clearly not dogmatism but aestheticism that was the danger.[5]

Assigning Cranmer to the aesthete category, for whom beauty of language stands above truth, it should not be unanticipated for Auden to understand how former Archbishop Cranmer, in the face of possible execution by being burned at the stake, chose initially to recant his beliefs. When Cranmer witnessed Reformationist colleagues perishing by auto-da-fé, it is said he reacted by "tearing off his cap, falling to his knees and desperately bewailing what was happening."[6] Fearing the prospects of such a death, the aesthete may recant his beliefs, which, to him, are formed only by the meaning of words. And yet, when it counted, at the moment of his own auto-da-fé martyrdom at the hands of the papist monarch, Mary, and her minions, Cranmer chose to recant his previous recantation.

Auden admits his own failings in this respect, using the Book of Common Prayer for purposes of an example, as the aesthete who may pay less attention to the meaning of the words and more to their beauty when strung together canorously and effectively:

---

5. Ibid., 30–31.
6. MacCulloch, *Thomas Cranmer*, 582.

Those of us who are Anglicans, know well that the language of the Book of Common Prayer, its extraordinary beauties of sound and rhythm, can all too easily tempt us to delight in the sheer sound without thinking about what the words mean, or whether we mean them.[7]

Auden also plays with the notion: Would Cranmer, as a man of words, an aesthete, have withheld his recantation of his initial recantation should his life have been spared? Or did the impending execution at the stake actually cause Cranmer to become even more certain of a decision to recant his earlier recantation? None of us can know the final and true answer to these questions, but Auden leads us through the drama toward a possible conclusion that the initial recantation would have stuck if Cranmer had been spared the martyrdom. ("If the Pope had bid me live, I should have served him," wrote Williams, placing this conclusion in the mouth of the Cranmer character.) Cranmer, however, being a man of words, stood by those words and suffered death as a result, insistent the hand that had first recanted by signature, "which wrote the contrary of God's will in me, since it offended most, shall suffer first."[8]

We've already discussed Auden's fascination with Charles Williams, the author of *Thomas Cranmer of Canterbury*. It's likely that Cranmer represented a near equally captivating individual for Auden. Considering the acknowledged respect Auden held for Cranmer's writing and skill in compiling the Book of Common Prayer, and the evident familial and personal connections that Auden obviously felt toward the Anglican Church, one must wonder why he wrote little about Cranmer. That is also a question for which we have no answer. It should be noted, however, that the preceding August 1967, he had written a shorter version of his comments for the magazine *Holiday* that would later be presented in the Eliot lecture about the Williams play.[9]

---

7. Auden, *Secondary Worlds*, 40.

8. Ibid., 44.

9. W. H. Auden, "By the Grace of God and Henry Tudor, Archbishop," *Holiday*, August 1967, in Edward Mendelson, ed., *The Complete Works of W. H. Auden Prose, Volume V, 1963–1968* (Princeton, NJ: Princeton University Press, 2015), 341–47.

Auden appears to have written even less on Miles Coverdale. Nonetheless, Auden arrives back in New York after delivering the T. S. Eliot lectures, palpably inspired to defend both Cranmer and Coverdale to the teeth, whose words he felt were seriously under attack by an overreaching set of American priests set on liturgical mischief. Auden had also taken an opportunity in the lecture on the Williams play to relate Cranmer's liturgical reform efforts to those that were then afoot in the late 1960s within the Episcopal Church. I do not think it particularly speculative to assume Auden had knowledge already of the Episcopal Church's reform plans; otherwise, he would not have used the phrase of "then and today" within the following comments:

> Cranmer was a priest and an artist, and like all artistic priests, then and today, he overestimated the spiritual importance of liturgical reform, and underestimated the resistance of the uneducated laity to it.[10]

So, what do these words tell us? They say that when Auden returned to the United States, the trial liturgy may have been "appalling" to him, but it was certainly not a surprise. I think he would have been more deeply surprised, had he lived for a few years more, by the rather favorable response that the Episcopal laity gave to the revisions in the Book of Common Prayer published in 1979. Yes, there were pockets of serious resistance by those who abandoned altogether the mainstream Episcopal Church as a result of the new liturgy, but only a handful of parishes in the United States actually took that extreme step. Not to be overly critical of Auden's prognosis, it is important to keep in mind that there had been no major overhaul of Cranmer's prayer book for the first four hundred years of its existence, and Auden's expectation for the possibility of an eruptive, countervailing riposte could have been shaped by the simple fact that the resistance to liturgical reform in response to Cranmer's first prayer book was so virulent in some quarters of

---

10. Auden, *Secondary Worlds*, 39.

England that the violent reaction became known as the Prayer Book Rebellion, which resulted in thousands of English perishing. Auden undoubtedly didn't expect that kind of response to the Episcopal Church's revision to the Book of Common Prayer, but, at the same time, I do think Auden believed opposition among Episcopalians would be more severe than it ultimately proved to be.

The month following W. H. Auden's death in September 1973, an article by him appeared in *Vogue* entitled, "I Have a Ferocious Bee in My Bonnet," in which he discusses his considerable displeasure with the "contemporary liturgical reforms and new translations of the Bible."[11] The exact language he uses for a good portion of the article is drawn from his July 6, 1971 letter to me, which we've already considered, and to a lesser extent from his letter of March 19, 1968 to Canon Charles Guilbert, which will be examined in the next chapter. The key points he raises in the article are: the King James Bible and the Book of Common Prayer were compiled "at exactly the right moment, when the English language had already become more or less what it is today and when there was a 'feeling for the ritual and ceremonious which today we have almost entirely lost'"; the desirability of retranslating the prayer book back into Latin; and the need to employ a dead language for the Rite, which is his language for the Eucharist, and which Auden characterizes as "the link between the dead and the unborn." He also criticizes the prosaic and misleading nature of some recently translated biblical texts and ends with a strong indictment of both Roman Catholics and Episcopalians for confirming children at a young age: "To confirm children sometime between the ages of eleven and fourteen, as the Roman Catholics and Episcopalians usually do, is absurd, for no child is capable of making a personal commitment."[12]

Of course, Auden's perspectives on all the matters covered in the *Vogue* article deserve attention, but we should respect the

---

11. W. H. Auden, "I Have a Ferocious Bee in My Bonnet," *Vogue*, October 1973, in Mendelson, ed., *The Complete Works of W. H. Auden Prose, Volume VI, 1969–1973*, 632.

12. Ibid.

reality that as he came to the end of his life, the subjects that seemed to carry considerable weight for him included liturgical texts, about which he had committed much intellectual and emotional energy since the latter part of the 1960s. At approximately the same time he also decides to turn, in the Eliot lectures, to two personally appealing and consequential figures, Charles Williams and Thomas Cranmer, both of whom he admits had been seminal influences on him and had helped shape crucial elements of his internal and external identities: the first, the language of his spirituality (Anglican Christianity), and the latter, language for his poetry.

Shortly before his death, Auden does spend a paragraph on Miles Coverdale and on Psalm 42, as an aside in a review of a church hymnary, published June 29, 1973 in the *New Statesman*:

> A digression. Since I was brought up on it, I resent any alterations to Coverdale, but then, since I know no Hebrew, I do not notice when he mistranslates. Thus, I understand that the phrase, "because of the noise in the water-pipes" really means the noise, presumably faint, made by underground streams in a limestone country. But when I was young it gave the organist such a wonderful opportunity to make his instrument roar.[13]

Inasmuch as Auden accepted the realization that changes to Coverdale's psalms were necessary to correct mistranslations, he himself proposed an alteration for Psalm 42, which was acceptable to the drafting committee, for Coverdale's term "water-pipes," replacing the word with "cataracts." Because of Auden's familiarity from childhood with "faint" water noises from underground streams in a limestone country, which displayed itself through his famous poem, "In Praise of Limestone," it is somewhat baffling that "cataracts" was chosen since its meaning conveys a flood, waterfall, downpour, or steep rapids, certainly producing a louder noise than

---

13. W. H. Auden, "Praiseworthy," *New Statesman*, June 29, 1973, in Mendelson, ed., *The Complete Works of W. H. Auden Prose, Volume VI, 1969–1973*, 619.

merely a "faint" sound. One wonders why he did not suggest the word "murmur," which he used to communicate the phenomenon of the sound of faint underground streams, as he had done to end "In Praise of Limestone":

> . . . what I hear is the murmur /Of underground streams, what
> I see is a limestone landscape.[14]

—or even, perhaps, its gerund, "murmuring." Nonetheless, the Episcopal Psalter was only one of several translations that chose the word "cataracts" for the phenomenon of those water noises in Psalm 42.

At this point, it is important to look at the poetry of W. H. Auden for insights into other subject areas where "The Crucibles" and Auden shared common interests, lest we forget that he appears to have authored no poems on either Thomas Cranmer or Miles Coverdale. This conclusion is not meant to suggest that the paths taken by the Reformationists did not intersect with Auden's verse, for a nexus certainly existed in other areas we shall soon examine. An Auden sonnet that has relevance in this respect is *Luther*. The poem dwells more on Luther's personality than it does on the prominent convictions of the Protestant Reformation, but the poem's two alluding lines from the third quatrain,

> "All Works, Great Men, Societies are bad.
> The Just shall live by Faith . . ." he cried in dread.[15]

open a huge vista onto the reformers' theological world, a world that would have occupied the focus of Thomas Cranmer and Miles Coverdale. In 1517, Luther—cleric, teacher, and former monk—then in his mid-thirties, had tacked his ninety-five theses on the church door in Wittenberg, soon after hearing from local people who listened to a traveling Dominican preacher with the mission of selling indulgences for the Catholic Church announce: "there

---

14. W. H. Auden, *Collected Shorter Poems, 1927–1957*, 241.
15. Ibid., 193.

was no sin so great that it would not be absolved thereby, even if, as they say, taking an impossible example, a man should violate the mother of God."[16]

". . . [A] man is justified by faith . . ."[17] Luther had read from the Apostle Paul and ". . . certainly it is by faith alone that we are saved" from Augustine.[18] The Apostle had also penned: "For by grace you have been saved through faith; and this is not your own doing, it is the gift of God—not because of works."[19]

Good works shall follow, but it all, justification and redemption, begins with individual faith—that is what Luther and the Reformationists had heard. The power of Augustine's confessional and tortuous journey to conversion and his generative and regenerative doctrine of faith as the source for justification and redemption were compelling for the Reformationists, who held numerous and immoderate reasons for rejecting the institutional organism of the papacy, while accepting the beliefs of some of its doctors. As a result, many Reformationists chose to identify themselves as Augustinians. Auden was probably a bit of an Augustinian himself, especially when it came to the mutual dislike of Manicheans, whose *weltanschauung* Auden had often mocked, a dislike he shared with Augustine, who had, before his conversion, been inclined toward the Manichean point of view. If the institution and its stewards of the papacy were corrupt, as in Auden's words portraying Luther:

> He saw the Devil busy in the wind,
> Over the chiming steeples and then under
> The doors of nuns and doctors who had sinned,[20]

then there was much for the Reformationists to do to rid the children of God of Catholicism and to effect an individual's direct

---

16. Williams, *The Descent of the Dove*, 166.

17. The Holy Bible, New Testament (San Francisco: Ignatius Press, 1966), 140.

18. St. Augustine, *On Faith and Works* (New York and Mahwah, NJ: The Newman Press, 1988), 34.

19. The Holy Bible, New Testament, 175.

20. Auden, *Collected Shorter Poems, 1927–1957*, 193.

relationship with God (i.e., a vernacular liturgy and vernacular Bible; elimination of false adoration that isolates the worshiper from the Worshiped; removal of fictitious relics and the principle of transubstantiation; and acceptance of election, among other curatives). Auden would additionally take up this theme again of Luther and "faith and works" in the longer poem "Letter to Lord Byron."

Auden had much to say about the Protestant Reformation. It is clearly a subject to which he had given much attention and thought. I do not think he ever fully reconciled his liturgical attraction to higher church practices, however, such as those that had been exercised by Catholicism, with the more flexible habitat of the Anglican/Episcopal religion and its practice and tenets of the Anglican compromise. Repeatedly, Auden proclaimed he was an Episcopalian, but he often espoused preferences that didn't align themselves that way. In a June 1960 review in *The Mid-Century* of *Young Man Luther*, the well-regarded analytical work by Erik Erikson, Auden offers these insights about the Reformation, which had given birth to the Anglican Church:

> The Protestant Era might be called the era of the Rebellious Son, but this rebellion was against the Fathers. . . . Protestantism set out to replace the collective external voice of tradition by the internal voice of the individual conscience. . . . In religion, it shifts the emphasis from the human reason, which is a faculty we share with our neighbors, and the human body, which is capable of partaking with other human bodies in the same liturgical acts, to the human will which is unique and private to every individual.[21]

Later, in the same review, he states he believes the Protestant Era is now over and that we have entered a Catholic Era in which, unlike Protestantism, there will be less emphasis on the concept that:

---

21. W. H. Auden, "Greatness Finding Itself," *The Mid-Century*, June 1960, in Mendelson, ed., *The Complete Works of W. H. Auden Prose, Volume IV, 1956–1962*, 286.

. . . every human being, irrespective of family, class, or occu-
pation, is unique before God; the complementary and equally
Christian doctrine emphasized by Catholicism is that we are
all members, one with another, both in the Earthly and the
Heavenly City.[22]

Over the last fifty years, his prediction has not come to pass.
However, it is relevant to recognize that Auden made these comments at a time when the collective idea was valued, especially in
liberal quarters, more than it is today. Communism had not run its
course in 1960, when the governmental collectives of socialism and
communism still represented a more prominent socio-economic
force in many parts of the world. It would not have been unexpected
for this collective motif that Auden envisioned at the time to affect
the religious community as well. Ironically, evangelical Protestantism, rather than adhering to the thematic emphasis on individual
conscience, has proven Auden partially correct (but for the opposite branch of his argument)—with its own vigorous march over
the course of the last several decades toward collective ideology
and collective political activism, certainly as experienced in the
United States.

In addition to those mentioned above in this chapter and in
chapter three, there are other examples of conceptual intersections
between W. H. Auden and "The Crucibles" in his verse. The next
two excerpts are taken from his *Collected Shorter Poems*, published
in 1967:

. . . these are our Common Prayer,[23] (from "In Praise of Limestone")

They whispered still of most unsocial fires,
Though Crown and Mitre warned their silly flocks . . .[24]
   (from "Bucolics")

---

22. Ibid., 289.

23. Auden, *Collected Shorter Poems, 1927–1957*, 240.

24. Ibid., 257.

The following excerpts are taken from the *Collected Longer Poems*, published in 1969:

> For since the British Isles went Protestant
> A church confession is too high for most.[25] (from "Letter to Lord Byron")

> My grandfathers on either side agree
> In being clergymen and C. of E.[26] (from "Letter to Lord Byron")

> We cannot, then, will Heaven where
> Is perfect freedom. . . .[27] (from "New Year Letter")

The term "perfect freedom" is a phrase of the *Collect for Peace* from the 1549 Book of Common Prayer[28] and remains as part of Morning Prayer Services in *A Collect for Peace* contained in the current edition.[29]

The following excerpts from the poetry of W. H. Auden were taken from *W. H. Auden, Collected Poems*, edited by Edward Mendelson:

> "Make me chaste, Lord, but not yet."[30] (from "The Love Feast")

The theology of the Reformationists owed much to St. Augustine. The above Auden verse line from "The Love Feast" is a witticism drawn from Augustine's *Confessions*.[31]

> . . . Not like the others, not like our dear dumb friends
> Who, poor things, have nothing to hide,
> Not, thank God, like our Father either
> From whom no secrets are hid.[32] (from "Secrets")

---

25. Auden, *Collected Longer Poems*, 38.

26. Ibid., 67.

27. Ibid., 107.

28. 1549 Book of Common Prayer, Seconde Collect for Peace.

29. The Book of Common Prayer, 99.

30. W. H. Auden, *Collected Poems*, Edward Mendelson, ed., Modern Library Edition (New York: Random House, 2007), 612.

31. Saint Augustine, *Confessions* (Oxford: Oxford University Press, 2008), 145.

32. Auden, *Collected Poems*, 621.

The above verse line, "From whom no secrets are hid," is a clause from the opening sentence of the opening collect of the Communion service, as it appeared in the 1549 Book of Common Prayer.[33] The clause has been brought forward, slightly adjusted as "from you no secrets are hid," and is also part of the current Episcopal Book of Common Prayer in the introduction to The Holy Eucharist Rite Two.[34]

> Luther & Zwingli
> Should be treated singly:
> L hated the Peasants,
> Z the Real Presence.[35] (from "Academic Graffiti")

> There's no *We* at an instant,
> Only *Thou* and *I*, two regions
> of protestant being which nowhere overlap: . . .[36]
> (from "Thanksgiving for a Habitat")

Other and additional quotes from the verse of W. H. Auden could have been chosen to underscore the concentric and cogent linkage between Auden and "The Crucibles." These examples are, however, enough to make the point that hardly needs to be made: Auden routinely drew on traditional language, theological history, thematic constellations, and textual context from the prayer book and Bible, as adjusted to his own special scope and detail, for the body and inspiration of material that gave direction, purpose, and definition to the broad dimensions of his often eloquent verse.

---

33. 1549 Book of Common Prayer, The Supper of the Lorde, and the holy Communion, commonly called the Masse.
34. The Book of Common Prayer, 355.
35. Auden, *Collected Poems*, 681.
36. Ibid., 713.

∽

CHAPTER 7

Dear Canon Guilbert from W. H. Auden

W. H. AUDEN AND CANON CHARLES GUILBERT held quite different views on rendering an updated version of the psalms. To Guilbert, while the genius and beauty of the past Coverdale version should lead the way, recent scholarship and more accurate and contemporary expressions of old revelations can more easily open minds to the exploration of uncommon experiences of those who came before us. To Auden, the more recognizably pleasing, the more ceremonial and formal poetic language—in this case, the sixteenth-century Coverdale retranslation—should retain its fully traditional elevation, thus verging on the magical and even unconditionally insightful. For him, such language can still speak to us personally and persuasively with gravitas. The existence of these two arguments is not unique to our age. As previously mentioned, the 1660s was a time for a similar debate when some proposed the more recent King James version of the psalms be included in the Book of Common Prayer, rather than the older version of Miles Coverdale; the older, in that case, won the hour.

There is one point, however, on which Guilbert and Auden could agree: those of us who are incidentally part of the twentieth and twenty-first centuries have a duty, a right, and a privilege to step back to a different age in order to help us understand and explore our own human spirituality, both as a people and as individuals. In the midst of all that is happening in our personal and pluralistic, near and distant worlds, it is both mysterious and non-contextual that we should choose to reach back in time approximately three thousand years when the first psalms were being written in northern Israel; and yet, we do reach back regularly to the poetry of this ancient people, unsophisticated and uneducated by our standards, "stiff-necked," according to the Book of Exodus, to give us insights into our own postmodern spirituality. This regular, but preternatural phenomenon of looking back for past expressions of enlightenment tends to give further justification to the words of Auden, who wrote, as a virtually throwaway line in the middle of a general correspondence between us about what was appealing in the modern context: "I don't believe there is such an animal as Twentieth Century Man."[1]

When the winds and predicates of war begin to resound in ambient voices after the Sunday service at coffee hour, in ad hoc sermons from guest speakers, and in utterances rising energetically from the pages of liturgical literature, it is time for the War Department to formulate rebuttal plans and resilient, cohesive retaliation. By the time W. H. Auden attended church services in the fall of 1967 at his neighborhood Episcopal parish, St. Mark's in-the-Bowery, he already knew changes to the traditional liturgy of the Episcopal Church were imminent and probably inevitable, and he had developed his arguments for a counterattack.

After attending services one Sunday morning that had featured a new, experimental liturgy in anticipation of possible adoption by the country's Episcopal churches, Auden penned a four-paragraph letter to his parish priest, Father J. C. Michael Allen, dated November 20, 1967, that embodied propositions that would be part of subsequent attacks in letters to Canon Guilbert and to me. Edward Mendelson would, in a note to me, call Auden's letter to Father Allen the letter "that started it all."[2]

---

1. Letter to J. Chester Johnson from W. H. Auden, dated July 6, 1971.
2. Letter to J. Chester Johnson from Edward Mendelson, dated July 2, 1999.

Auden had the issue in his sights and was ready. He asked Father Allen whether he had "gone stark raving mad," and he called the new liturgy "appalling." In addition, he stated that "Our Church" (meaning the Anglican Church with the Episcopal Church being the American branch) had the singular "good-fortune" of having its prayer book composed at exactly the right time (i.e., late enough for the language to be intelligible for a modern person and early enough when people had an instinctive feeling for the formal and ceremonious, essential for liturgical language—an attribute that has been "almost totally lost"). He referred to the problems with which the Roman Catholics were struggling in the writing of their vernacular mass, and he asked that the liturgical practices stick with the traditional Book of Common Prayer and the King James Bible. Further, he emphasized that liturgy keeps "us in touch with the past and the dead." The exception for preaching is the same he used four years later in the July 6, 1971 letter.[3] The suggestion of liturgy keeping us in touch with the dead is also consistent with the language Auden enlisted in the same 1971 letter, though for the latter, he added "the unborn" to "the dead" being affected by liturgy.[4] The "good-fortune" argument is repeated shortly thereafter in a March 19, 1968 letter to Canon Guilbert.[5]

Weighing the constancy with which Auden retained these elements of his arguments in subsequent writings, it should be quite obvious he had given considerable thought to the reasoning he would articulate for his opposition, even before he wrote Father Allen. Auden's views on the new Episcopal liturgy would undoubtedly gather scrutiny since he had access to outlets through which he could voice contrary and credible opinions, and it is therefore not surprising that his letter to Father Allen made its way, within only a month, into the hands of the Church's Standing Liturgical Commission.

---

3. Letter to Rev. J. C. Michael Allen from W. H. Auden, dated November 20, 1967.

4. Letter to J. Chester Johnson from W. H. Auden, dated July 6, 1971.

5. Letter to Canon Guilbert from W. H. Auden, dated March 19, 1968. Courtesy of the Archives of the Episcopal Church.

In turn, Canon Guilbert sent a letter on behalf of the Commission to Auden on December 20, 1967. Canon Guilbert responded to Auden's note with two principal purposes in mind. First and foremost, Guilbert invited Auden to become a member of the drafting committee on the Psalter. Second, the letter reacted to Auden's comments to Father Allen. Guilbert requested an opportunity to discuss the reasons for Auden's characterization of the new liturgy as appalling. Since Auden went out of his way to criticize specifically the change in the phrase "the quick and the dead" to "the living and the dead" as part of the Nicene Creed, Guilbert proceeded to defend the action by portraying the word "quick" as obsolete and by stating that the adjustment achieved "from the standpoint of prosody—breaking a string of anapests that almost establish a metrical pattern with a fourth paean." (I believe Canon Guilbert meant "paeon" instead of "paean.") While Auden apparently never returned in writing to a discussion of Guilbert's defense of the change, I'm inclined to think, based on Auden's knack for monosyllabicity in quite a few of his own verses, he would have argued against the substitution of a bi-syllabic word that altered the full monosyllabic run or movement in the phrase "the quick and the dead." In any case, we cannot know for certain his poetic problems with the change.

Canon Guilbert also indicated he and others on the Standing Liturgical Commission agreed with Auden's conclusion that liturgy requires ceremonious and formal language, stating that the weight of Auden's opinion, in this respect, would be appreciated. Guilbert described the approach that the Psalter Committee had taken toward the retranslation, and he made it clear that Auden's membership on the committee would not preclude him from "seeing, studying, and commenting on all of the liturgical materials the Commission through its several committees will be working on during the coming nine years."[6]

Auden received the Guilbert letter the next day and immediately replied with a short note dated December 22, 1967. His views

---

6. Letter to W. H. Auden from Canon Guilbert, dated December 20, 1967. Courtesy of the Archives of the Episcopal Church.

on aspects of the prayer book revision process are further clarified in the several written communications to Canon Guilbert; however, it is rather curious, based on the extensiveness of his letter to Father Allen, that Auden would choose not to comment on any of the specific issues raised by Canon Guilbert: the desire of Guilbert to follow up on Auden's use of the term "appalling"; the adjustment explained by Guilbert from "the quick" to "the living" in the Creed; the mutual agreement on the nature of liturgical language being ceremonious and formal; the Psalter Committee's approach to its work; and the ability of Auden, if he so wished, to review the work produced by other committees working on other aspects of the revision of the Book of Common Prayer. The reply to Guilbert's letter was short and sweet. Auden agreed to serve on the Psalter Committee. Indeed, his response to that particular issue was stunningly expansive: "I should be honored and delighted to serve in any capacity on the Standing Liturgical Commission," though with a warning—he'd always be in Europe during the summer.[7]

The third and final sentence of the short reply to Guilbert consisted of a reference to an attachment that would set forth "a few reflections on the liturgical situation in the Episcopal Church as I, probably foolishly, see it." The attachment contained a series of ruminations and insights entitled "Liturgy and Time." There were two major subjects covered in the piece. First, Auden amplified considerably several of the topics mentioned in the Father Allen letter; at the same time, he opened new fields for debate. In particular, Auden enlarged the commentaries on the fortuitous timing that had existed for the composition of the Book of Common Prayer in the sixteenth century and explained that though "certain words have changed their meaning, no sensible hearer is misled" by the changes. In his words, "had it been King Alfred instead of Henry VIII who revolted against the Pope and ordered his bishops to compose a Book of Common Prayer, we should not to-day be able to understand a word of it."

---

7. Letter to Canon Guilbert from W. H. Auden, dated December 22, 1967.

Auden stressed that sixteenth-century writers had more of an "instinctive feeling for formal and ceremonious speech," and he again reviewed the "unfortunate position" that the Roman Church faced in developing a vernacular liturgy. He also underscored an idea that he would discuss later: "There may be points at which the translators made mistakes, which must, of course, be corrected, but why to re-write the whole thing?" In a related comment, he warns current translators not "to have the impudence to believe we can write better liturgical English than Cranmer." In addition to a reiteration of early ground he had plowed in the Father Allen letter, he plowed new rows with the proposition that liturgy should, by its nature, be conservative and not subject to continuous adaptation or adjustment, for "we are individual members of the common human race, with the same needs at all times and in all places." Auden also offers the thesis that "vernacular liturgy" had its basis in the conversion of barbaric peoples after Christianity became an official State religion, and because conversion was not a personal choice, there remained at that time a great gulf between the priest and laity. To him, if the spiritual and temporal authorities had taught every barbarian convert enough Latin (or Greek) to understand the original liturgy, there would have been no need for a vernacular one. For the first time in these dialogues, we see reference to an act in a present time (i.e., the Eucharist) being a bridge "between the dead and the unborn"—a concept to which Auden returns later. He makes an associated argument to which he does not return when he addresses analogous territory. In this more subtle aspect, Auden refers to the Incarnation, Passion, and Resurrection of Christ as definite acts within history, and since "time is not an illusion," any act or liturgy that repeats such historical events will also tie the future and the past. He commented on the danger of heretical outcomes from careless translations. To wit, he recounted a story of the time he had spoken at Westminster Abbey on the biblical scripture found in Romans 8: a mistranslation of a key word in the reading had turned a certain important concept into a "purely manichean notion," which the reader is left to conclude Auden thought heretical.[8]

It has proven to be a fascinating exercise to follow Auden's thinking on the Episcopal Church's retranslation program for the psalms. He remained relatively restrained in his criticism of that part of the revision of the Book of Common Prayer. In sum, he stressed that Coverdale should be maintained except where mistranslations had occurred, and he admitted, on occasion, that there were indeed mistakes that needed to be corrected. Further, Auden argued that even if mistranslations occurred there would be no need to rewrite the entirety of Coverdale. Of course, it was never the committee's intent to rewrite completely the Coverdale version, based on the history and judgments I gleaned during my time spent on the retranslation of the psalms. Auden appears to have concluded that to be the case and that he could, in a significant way, agree with parts of the committee's approach so that the psalm revisions would not be a constant nemesis. Anyone with a fair and appreciative eye for the psalms contained in the 1979 Book of Common Prayer would have to conclude the essential character and flow of Coverdale have been maintained and his words and themes still resonate and echo. Nonetheless, Auden complained that the modern translations of the psalms didn't sound like poetry.

The second major area covered by these ruminations examined the proposed revised liturgy of the Mass (Eucharist). Interestingly enough, however, it was for the revised Eucharist that he often targeted his most vitriolic attacks. That being the case, Auden's remarks were quite subdued in his piece, "Liturgy and Time," unlike his later barrages. Reading his impassioned pieces on the Eucharistic revisions in other contexts, the striking mildness of his comments contained on the subject under "Liturgy and Time" causes one to blink a few times in anticipation of a pending verbal onslaught, but none comes. In many ways, the discussion here seems to stay intentionally clear of hot and heavy issues, and away

---

8. Ibid.

from assaults over certain language. Rather, Auden attends to the order of the Mass; interestingly enough, the Auden term "Mass," which is not employed in the 1979 Book of Common Prayer, is a return to the Catholic expression and a term Cranmer, based on his actions in the 1552 prayer book, would have demonstrably opposed. Auden concentrates on the importance of the various components of the Eucharist, as he suspects those items have been given criticality by the Episcopal drafters, though he touches lightly on specific phraseology related principally to theological issues. Surprisingly, he begins this part of his commentary by congratulating the Church for its decision in its preliminary drafts to include both a lesson from the Old Testament and a psalm, remarking that "few people any longer attend Matins or Evensong, so that, unless these are introduced," the congregation will never have an opportunity to hear anything read from the Old Testament. With generous words, he remarks, "I approve heartily."[9]

Auden then moves into a section he entitles "Objections" to items included in the preliminary draft on the Eucharist. He complains that the General Confession and the Prayer of Humble Access are relegated to an optional status and proceeds to discuss the reasons that "a public expression of penitence before approaching the altar is essential." Next, he takes issue with the feature of the "we believe" language in the Nicene Creed, saying that "nobody can do my believing for me: the adult church is a community, not a mob." He then encourages the Episcopal Church not to omit the *Filioque* clause in the Nicene Creed: "[I]f the doctrine of the Holy Trinity is accepted, then the double procession of the Holy Ghost from the Father <u>and</u> the Son is a necessary corollary." Noting that the Greek Orthodox Church does not accept the *Filioque* clause in the Creed, Auden then explains his belief that their refusal is one of politics tied to a rejection of the conquerors who imposed their beliefs strictly on the basis of force. He also discusses his own inability to believe in either the Immaculate Conception or the Assumption of Mother Mary and then unexpectedly turns to

---

9. Ibid.

examine a subject quite separate from the Eucharist through an encouragement of the Episcopal Church to understand that ecumenical agreements should take into account honest differences of opinion: "[W]e have to begin by saying on certain points of doctrine we disagree. . . ." He also decides to weigh in on prayers, describing his recommendations for whom parish churches should pray publicly and justifying his criticism of the approach taken on this matter in the preliminary draft document then being circulated by the Episcopal Church, declaring, "But when it comes to praying for all sorts and conditions of men, the 'democratically-minded' compilers of the new prayer, have gone mad." He proceeds to take strong exception to the Church's examples.

Twice in this chapter have we encountered Auden applying the word "mad" to liturgical circumstances that especially piqued him. It is noteworthy and coincidental that Cranmer, hundreds of years earlier, was attracted, to a similar degree, to the same word for special effect. In the letter to Father Allen, Auden asked his parish priest whether he had "gone stark raving mad" utilizing a trial liturgy. In the most recent example, Auden conscripts "mad" to lambast compilers of a new, but irksome prayer.

While over four hundred years separated the uses of "mad" by these two writers, the characterization, emphasized placement, and relative intensity of the word for the situations are eerily similar. The two instances that are presented for which Cranmer chooses to embrace "mad" consist of excerpts from his Preface to Coverdale's 1540 Great Bible, as follows:

> "And we in this (sayeth he) be not unlyke to them that beeying mad sette theyr own houses on fyre, and that slay theyr owne chyldren, or beate theyr owne parentes."
> ". . . I would marvaile muche that any man should be so mad, as to refuse in darkenes, lyght: in honger foode: in cold fyre:"

Through these remarkable comparisons, one can envision Thomas Cranmer at Auden's shoulder almost audibly intimating the word "mad" that Cranmer invoked so effectively in 1540.

Auden concludes with a minor point that "Cranmer was litur-
gically right in altering the Roman order and putting the 'Gloria'
after communion. The Roman mass peters out undramatically."[10]
The "Gloria" is a major doxology that begins: "Glory to God on
high, and in earth peace, good will toward men." Auden sent "Liturgy and Time" to Canon Guilbert in late 1967, and twelve years
passed before the revised Book of Common Prayer would actually
be published by the Episcopal Church. By that time, several issues
raised by Auden, such as the public prayers and the position of
"Gloria" in the communion, had taken an entirely different course
for the prayer book and were no longer subject to the same dimensions Auden had given to them.

It is simply not possible to know whether W. H. Auden would
have approved of the final decisions by the Standing Liturgical
Commission and the Episcopal Church at large on the elements of
his objections, but I think he would have been reasonably pleased
with at least the handling of the Confession and the *Filioque*, if
not the prayers. Moreover, the decision of the Church to allow an
optional choice by parishes of a Rite I Eucharist for congregations
that desired to adhere to the older forms of the Eucharist would
have appealed to Auden, though most churches in New York City,
which had been his winter home for many years, adopted, for the
most part, the more contemporary alternative Rite II.

There is an aphorism ascribed to the German philosopher
Johann Fichte which states that the kind of philosophy one has
depends on what kind of human being one is. The fulsome attacks
Auden aimed at the revisions to the Book of Common Prayer are,
of course, quite intriguing. His reaction to the planned revisions
was not a mere intellectual exercise or even a literary or spiritual
one, for that matter; rather, to my thinking, the illustrated intensity of emotion suggests something much more visceral and cul-
tural. It occurred to me long ago that Auden's Americanization
never reached the depths of T. S. Eliot's Britishization. In other

---

10. Ibid.

words, Eliot became more British than Auden became American. In rural Arkansas where I grew up, there is a saying that lots of folks spend half their lives trying to leave the place and the other half trying to get back. I've often felt that there may have been a little of that alive and well in Auden's relationship with Britain. After all, clear evidence exists that in the midst of Auden's participation in the revision of the Book of Common Prayer, he was contemplating the move back to his original homeland well before he actually made the final step to return.[11] Then, near the end of the summer in 1972, Auden cleaned out his New York apartment and changed his winter home at last to England, settling in at Oxford in October.[12]

I will not speculate on the extent to which his casting of eyes homeward during the years preceding his final move back to England affected his rankled views on the American adjustments to his beloved Book of Common Prayer, the book of worship he had used as a youngster when a choirboy, the book his grandfathers on both sides relied upon as Anglican clergymen. While it could be a bit presumptuous to let speculation run a thread too long in this direction, the elements should not be dismissed either. In the words of a former chairman of the Liturgical Commission for the Anglican Church, the Rt. Rev. David Stancliffe, explaining the criteria applied by the Anglican Church in authorizing Psalter texts for usage among Anglican churches: "The greatest influences were probably the subliminal ones. . . ."[13]

It is not as though the Episcopal Church traversed whole cloth across the Atlantic Ocean to stake out a wholly owned subsidiary of the Anglican Church. Indeed, the Episcopal Church emerged energetically out of the American Revolution and conformed with the break from England. At that time, many Anglican churches in America were burned, and some Anglican clergy forced to take the

---

11. Edward Mendelson, *Later Auden*, 506.

12. Ibid., 510.

13. E-mail to J. Chester Johnson from the Rt. Rev. David Stancliffe, dated October 13, 2014.

first ships back to England or scurry north to Canada. Moreover, the first American Episcopal bishop, Samuel Seabury, received consecration in November 1784, not from an Anglican bishop, but rather from three nonjuring Scottish bishops (those who refused to swear allegiance to the British) who were quite happy to take this action of contravention against the Church of England. In turn, Seabury agreed to recognize the legitimacy of the Scottish Episcopal Church and to advocate the use of its Eucharistic prayer, which was drawn from the 1549 Book of Common Prayer "rather than from the shortened form of the prayer in the 1552 edition and employed in all subsequent English editions."[14] There have been many issues for which the Episcopal Church in the United States and the Church of England took separate courses. For example, the Episcopal Church adopted the humanizing and liberalizing step of ordaining women to the priesthood two decades before the Church of England took a similar action in 1994. Emphasizing the point, the Episcopal Church chose a woman as its presiding bishop in 2006. As this book is being written, the Episcopal Church has just been sanctioned by the Anglican primates of the Anglican Communion, including the Church of England, for a period of three years as a result of the Episcopal Church's authorization of same-sex marriages.

Auden was mistaken to act as though the Episcopal Church could have somehow been as firmly aligned with the psalms that were associated with the 1549 Book of Common Prayer as the Church of England had been, taking into account the fact that the Episcopal Church made over a thousand changes to the Coverdale version for its own Book of Common Prayer in 1928. Furthermore, as several Irish and British writers—including Winston Churchill—have astutely pointed out: we are two countries separated by a common language and, in many respects, that commonality has often been illusory. England did not have a phenomenon to our Walt Whitman, whose poetic style and structures he characterized as

---

14. Robert W. Prichard, *A History of the Episcopal Church*, 120.

the "great exception," meaning the poetry truly broke with the past and, in his distinctive case, offered a new verse that mirrored a new nation and world. He was, in many ways, our very first American poet, though many British admired and praised his work. America has often gone its own way with language and poetry, and the Episcopal Psalter would be no different in certain key respects.

Two months after posting the December 1967 letter to Canon Guilbert, Auden sends a much shorter letter, dated February 21, 1968, indicating an inability to attend the March 1968 meeting of the Psalter drafting committee due to a scheduling conflict. He also takes the opportunity to criticize a report he had received from Guilbert that apparently was prepared by a group Auden identifies as philologists, asserting, "Thank you so much for sending me the 1966 Report which I have read with great disapproval."[15] In this letter, Auden states that while philologists are valuable, "they can seldom understand the problems of translating poetry from one language into another." In his opinion, the art of translation consists of the ability to know when to depart from the strict sense of the original and when to be literal. Auden concludes that the people responsible for the "Prayer Book Psaltery were astonishingly good translators." (One can assume he means Miles Coverdale, in particular.) Furthermore, he takes issue with the Psalter retranslation committee's conclusion that mistranslations exist in the six examples forwarded to him and identified as in need of change— apparently, the individual psalms to be reviewed at the upcoming meeting, which he would be unable to attend. Auden does write, "I dare say there are places in the Psaltery where genuine mistranslations occur and need to be corrected"—a crucial admission for him, considering the fact that he saw no adjustment to Coverdale as being necessary for the six examples that were deemed candidates for mistranslation and thus subject to retranslation by the committee. To Auden, only the obvious, more egregious mistranslations

---

15. Letter to Canon Guilbert from W. H. Auden, dated February 21, 1968. Courtesy of the Archives of the Episcopal Church.

ought to be subject to change from the Coverdale version: "Suppose, for example, the Hebrew word means <u>a pomegranate</u> and had been translated as <u>a tomato</u>, it should be changed."[16] On its face, Auden's example offers a simple, firm grounding for the purpose of retranslating Coverdale's Psalter, but in practice Auden's guideline was interpreted by the committee as being too unidirectional (i.e., for more automatic retention of Coverdale's language, even where other problems existed). Auden discernibly had more than a little support on the committee for several of his ideas; however, the contrast between that which should be retranslated literally and that which should not essentially came down to favorite lines—a rather personal, inexact test. Auden's notion was difficult for the committee to defend as a matter of principle.

Notwithstanding the specific contributions made by Auden to the retranslation of the Episcopal Psalter, I believe he thought his principal responsibility to be that of an alternative voice to the seemingly prevailing one that was intent on major revisions to the entirety of the Book of Common Prayer. A clue to this context can be found in this thoughtful and quite eloquent excerpt from his letter to Canon Guilbert of March 19, 1968, a letter that could constitute his most revelatory in their series of correspondence. As previously noted, Canon Guilbert, at the time this letter was written, was not only chair of the drafting committee for retranslation of the psalms, but also custodian of the Book of Common Prayer. I am reasonably sure Auden had this fact in mind when he wrote these words, since the concepts bear a consequence well beyond those that deal exclusively with the psalms and explain the basis of his fundamental aversion and literary concerns for the general revision of the Book of Common Prayer:

> We had the Providential good-fortune, a blessing denied to the Roman Catholics, that our Prayer Book was compiled at the ideal historical moment, that is to say, when the English Language

---

16. Ibid.

was already in all essentials the language we use now—nobody has any difficulty understanding Shakespeare's or Cranmer's English, as they have difficulty with Beowulf or Chaucer—at the same time, men in the Sixteenth and Seventeenth centuries still possessed what our own has almost totally lost, a sense for the ceremonial and ritual both in life and in language.[17]

Those closest to Auden clearly recognized his predilection for a healthy dose of the ceremonial in his life and work. Christopher Isherwood, a longtime Auden colleague and occasional literary collaborator, once jokingly remarked that Auden

> enjoyed a high Anglican upbringing . . . he is still much preoccupied with ritual, in all its forms. When we collaborate, I have to keep a sharp eye on him—or down flop the characters on their knees . . . If Auden had his way, he would turn every play into a cross between grand opera and high mass.[18]

The broader context of Auden's engagement not being strictly limited to the Psalter is consistent with his less global concerns about technical problems existing in the Coverdale psalms, as reflected in comments from a letter Auden wrote to me indicating he would "try to persuade the scholars not to alter Coverdale unless there is a definite mistranslation."[19] Later that year, Auden wrote to me again, with a little more zest, in July 1971, explaining more openly his literary views about the psalms:

> As for the psalms, they are poems, and to "get" poetry, it should, of course, be read in the language in which it was written. I myself, alas, know no Hebrew. All I know is that Coverdale reads like poetry, and the modern versions don't.[20]

---

17. Letter to Canon Guilbert from W. H. Auden, dated March 19, 1968.
18. Kirsch, *Auden and Christianity*, 14–15.
19. Letter to J. Chester Johnson from W. H. Auden, dated January 28, 1971.
20. Letter to J. Chester Johnson from W. H. Auden, dated July 6, 1971.

Still, when faced with irrefutable scholarship of recognizable mis-translations in Coverdale's version, Auden was enough of a scholar to accept, though grudgingly, various requisite changes.

In his letter of March 19, 1968 to Canon Guilbert, Auden is quite open about his willingness to let Coverdale run free in expanding beyond the actual Hebrew words to be translated. Bear in mind that when Auden speaks of the "Psaltery" in the following excerpt, it would be an equivalent term to mean Coverdale's psalms of the Book of Common Prayer.

> Most of (the) Psaltery's departures from the original, however, are clearly intentional elaborations which add something which is not in the Hebrew, but without contradicting it. I have yet to find an example where I do not feel that the elaboration is an enrichment, both in sense and rhythm.[21]

Auden would therefore allow Coverdale latitude, not for the sake of an accurate translation, but for the benefit of Coverdale's poetic style. The Grail version of the psalms, to which Auden refers below, had been published in 1963 and enlisted as a resource for the committee's work. For purposes of explaining further his position, Auden writes:

> I know no Hebrew, alas, so I must assume that the Grail version is the latest fruit of Biblical scholarship, the most literal English crib to the original Hebrew text at present available. All I can say about its makers is that they may know Hebrew very well, but, when it comes to their mother-tongue, they don't know their arse from a hole in the ground.[22]

A question arises, of course, as to the amount of latitude Auden would confer on Coverdale's translation techniques. In accordance with Auden's line of thinking, one could argue that a truly accurate rendering of the Hebrew is less critical than the sense of the

---

21. Letter to Canon Guilbert from W. H. Auden, dated March 19, 1968.
22. Ibid.

psalmist for an individual psalm. However, at what point do the embellishments ("enrichments," using Auden's word) occlude the true meaning of the psalmist? The Episcopal Psalter attempted to keep Coverdale as much as possible, except for obsolete wording and mistranslations, including instances where "enrichments" led to incorrect renderings and other considerations that will be examined later. There is no doubt that Auden would have taken a much less restricted view of what constituted enhancements or enrichments, as perpetrated by Coverdale, than the Psalter committee was willing to concede.

In substance, it may be wise not to see Auden and Guilbert (or the committee at large) at cross purposes, but rather to see their differences as reflective of the product each had in mind. For Auden, a more poetically attractive, more Elizabethan retranslation, at the risk of being somewhat less authentic and accurate, would prove suitable and sufficient, while Guilbert and the rest of the committee saw the product being something different, in terms of a more suitably correct rendering of the underlying verse. In truth, Auden didn't need to apply a new Episcopal Psalter to his own individual tastes, for he always had access to his beloved Coverdale should the motivation present itself. One knowledgeable member of the committee and observer of these conversations once suggested to me that on his deathbed, Auden would have surely reached for Coverdale of an early vintage. Since Auden died quite suddenly, we'll never know; the prediction, however, definitely contains a resounding ring of truth.

Other Auden preferences and thoughts, though less noteworthy, also appear in the March 19, 1968 letter to Canon Guilbert. For example, he confirmed his approval of the committee's proposed, more concrete word "rock" over Coverdale's abstraction, "strength," in Psalm 92:14. And for Psalm 122:3, he mentions his preference for the line of "Jerusalem is built as a city that is at unity in itself" to a much altered proposed version for the Episcopal Psalter; I'll discuss the outcome of that interplay very shortly. He also offers an insightful comment that the committee need be attentive to the proclivity in primitive epic poetry and song to the assumption that various human emotions are in fact "located in various organs of the body."[23]

Since I replaced Auden on the drafting committee and he and I never attended the same sessions, it was indispensable for me to rely on anecdotal information provided by other committee members to ascertain his contributions. I was, of course, very interested in the specific recommendations he would have made to the retranslation project, and I inquired during my time on the committee about those contributions. According to conversations I had with members of the committee, including Canon Guilbert, Auden provided three memorable contributions to our Psalter retranslation. The three versions of the psalms utilized for this comparison are Miles Coverdale's psalms of the 1540 Great Bible, the psalms of the 1928 edition of the Book of Common Prayer, and the psalms of the 1979 edition of the Book of Common Prayer. In Psalm 27, Auden replaced "secret place," which was carried in both Coverdale's 1540 Great Bible and the 1928 version, with "secrecy." For Psalm 42, he replaced "water pipes" in Coverdale's and "water floods" in the 1928 version with "cataracts." And for Psalm 95, the so-called Venite psalm, he replaced "prepared" in both Coverdale and the 1928 version with "molded." I also believe Auden made an additional and fourth gift to the retranslation: he presented strong arguments for the committee to retain a variety of inherited language. For example, I'm aware of his argument, set forth in writing to Canon Guilbert, for the preservation of this line from Psalm 122, as expressed in both Coverdale and the 1928 version: "Jerusalem is built as a city that is at unity in itself." With only one minor prepositional amendment, that is precisely the way the line now reads in the 1979 Book of Common Prayer. I'm sure there are other, more traditional lines or verses that were retained as a result of Auden's persuasive powers, though there are apparently no written notes to illustrate which ones he was able to preserve.

---

23. Ibid.

Canon Guilbert frequently voiced an opinion that Auden's negative response to the retranslation endeavor was a misinterpretation and that most of Auden's general "curmudgeonliness" about the Psalter retranslation—including his verbal suggestion, on occasion, that the best thing to be done to the psalms by the Episcopal Church, along with the rest of the Book of Common Prayer, would be to retranslate them back into Latin—had simply been in jest. For the Episcopal Psalter project, that is a more beneficial conjecture, but I think the discussions of his numerous and vehement commentaries contained in this book, specifically with respect to his defense of the sixteenth-century writers and the language produced by Coverdale, argue convincingly that Auden's stand cannot be discounted as an exercise in humor alone. Of course, his reputation for occasional flights of exaggeration in other settings remains legendary. Nevertheless, there can be no question he maintained an antagonism toward an expansive retranslation of Coverdale and an animus toward the larger revision of the Book of Common Prayer. The modulating factor that lessened his intensity toward the retranslation of the psalms consisted of the reality for numerous Coverdale mistranslations to be fixed at some point; after four hundred years, it was high time for the corrections to be made.

W. H. Auden died in September 1973, with the Episcopal Church's liturgical reform movement, in general, and the retranslation of the psalms, in particular, still in progress. It would be another six years before the revised Book of Common Prayer was formally released. During the years I served on the committee after Auden's death, members often invoked his name to stress an idea for one point or another. It was as though, in afterlife, he had not let go of his commitment to retain as much of the sixteenth-century language, style, and content as he could for the Book of Common Prayer. There's no question that the weight of his opinions caused the committee to be a bit more cautious about the elimination of Coverdale lines from the Episcopal Psalter, with the result that the spirit and actual words of Coverdale reside a little more thoroughly throughout the final rendition of the committee's work. Indeed, I will, now and then, even today, many decades later, hear Auden's sentences about the psalms in his letters both to Canon Guilbert and to me resonating in the moment and also causing me, on occasion, to shift nervously at the thought that maybe Coverdale deserved, during the committee's deliberations, a bit more attention for this psalm or that psalm.

There is one remaining question that has not been posed, let alone answered, about Auden and his letters to Canon Guilbert on the subjects examined in this chapter: Why did Auden's letters on these matters to Canon Guilbert abruptly end? Even though I do not know for sure, I have my suspicions that arise from a letter to me from Auden that I have yet to discuss. In 1971, the 92nd Street Y Poetry Center in New York City, where Auden had spoken and read his verse on numerous occasions, extended an invitation through me for members of the drafting committee to present a program on our retranslation. I contacted several committee members to request their attendance at the event. In response, Auden sent a two-sentence, handwritten note, dated June 14, 1971, stating he could not take part in the program; most telling was the second sentence, which had not been at all necessary, but which allowed Auden to vent his irritation at the entire revision project for the Book of Common Prayer: "For one thing, I'm so fed up with the whole liturgical reform nonsense that I am reduced to attending a Russian Orthodox Church."[24] At some earlier point, Auden had simply thrown up his hands in frustration; yet, he had one last flourish to give to the committee before letting it go. I would hear from him again in three weeks. Auden lived for more than another two years, but his final communication to the committee rested in the letter he sent to me, dated July 6, 1971.

---

24. Letter to J. Chester Johnson from W. H. Auden, dated June 14, 1971.

CHAPTER 8

⟳

Psalms for the 1979 Book of Common Prayer

Purpose, Principles, Process

N 1973, WHEN THE EPISCOPAL CHURCH issued interim psalms "for trial use," nine individuals were listed as members of the drafting committee. The list included W. H. Auden with an explanatory note that he had resigned as a result of his return to England in 1972; additionally, the list referred to an Episcopal bishop, who had resigned from the committee because of the press of diocesan work.[1] The remaining seven constituted the team that regularly met for the retranslation of the psalms—scholars with Latin, Greek, and Hebrew expertise, a musicologist, and a poet. Quite a few years separated me from the next youngest member of the committee until after the "trial use" psalms were issued and a new musicologist of approximately my age replaced an older one. During the residual years of the project, which drew to a close just prior to the final retranslated Psalter appearing in the 1979 Book of Common Prayer, the committee consistently relied on Canon Guilbert's proposed drafts for the psalms that were subject to retranslation at each working session, but with an eye toward the spreadsheet comparisons for verse lines I prepared from other recent Psalter revisions, consisting mainly of the Revised Standard

---

1. Guilbert, *The Prayer Book Psalter Revised*, I–II.

Version, the Grail psalms, the New English Bible, the American Bible, the Jerusalem Bible, and volumes on the psalms of the Anchor Bible. Of course, the 1928 Episcopal prayer book with its Coverdale preservation was continuously examined as an important source document. Five of the seven members have now passed on, leaving, in addition to me, James Litton, the committee's musicologist, who has enjoyed a highly productive and successful career as a conductor and writer of mostly classical and choral music.

When I first joined the committee, I soon noticed the Old Testament scholars, who dominated the committee by sheer numbers, were especially keen on producing rather literal renderings of the psalms—an approach that was certainly understandable, taking into account the disciplines in which they felt most comfortable. In fact, I had previously recognized this proclivity of the committee in the very first draft psalms I reviewed before sending off my initial letters of inquiry to Canon Guilbert, Auden, and Dentan. Over time, with the help of the line-by-line comparisons from other recent translations and retranslations, the committee responded to the obvious differences in the poetic results, the literary devices, and fluidity among the various revisions included in those comparisons. There's no question a discernible recognition of poetry as a priority took on prominence in our work, and Canon Guilbert, who held a demonstrable lyrical penchant anyway, did not hesitate in leading a charge in that direction. We'll take a look shortly at some prime examples of the changes of a poetic nature that occurred between the 1973 "trial use" version and the final 1979 Psalter.

In addition to Auden, several on the committee were also known writers in their own right, more often in their professional fields, but that wasn't solely the case, for there was considerable range in viewpoint and interests among the members. Even though some scholars on the committee admitted to a deep-seated admiration for Coverdale's retranslation and his familiar lines and phrases with which they had lived for years and which undoubtedly resonated in their heads and hearts, they did not exhibit any overarching loyalty to those lines and phrases that somehow prevented them from adequately remedying the shortcomings, mistranslations, or obsolescence, wherever appropriate. Notwithstanding the scholars' appreciation for the sounds of Coverdale's words, they certainly were, as a group, insistent adherents to scriptural accuracy—whether in the incremental stages of the "received text" (i.e., from Hebrew to Septuagint, Septuagint to Old Latin, Old Latin to Jerome, etc.), discussed in more detail below, or in the results of direct renderings from Hebrew to the finalized wording for each psalm.

Since publication of our work, I have spoken at a number of Episcopal churches and cathedrals about the Psalter in the 1979 Book of Common Prayer. At the conclusion of my presentation, I routinely entertain questions, and the inquiries from the audience often focus around adjustments to a word or two from a former favorite passage, an agreeable episode with one or more of our psalms in private or in a group setting, or an inquiry about W. H. Auden's participation and attitude. For the latter, I always stick closely to his statements and pronouncements on the subject that have now become public and on his correspondence to me, but I also cite the energy he exerted and devoted to the moment, particularly to the larger revision of the Book of Common Prayer, toward the end of his life and the imaginative, robust, if unconventional alternatives he proposed for the Episcopal program, both for the psalms and for the entirety of the prayer book revision. The most surprising aspect of those audience responses to my presentations has been the absence of criticism for our work—general congratulatory and thankful appreciation has come our way ("our" since I inevitably represent in those settings the committee as a whole). Maybe, this laudatory reply is not a good thing. Maybe, it's purely a function of good manners. Maybe, it's just respect for the enormous effort that went into the endeavor. Maybe, it's a bit of pride that other branches of the Anglican Communion and the Lutherans in the United States and Canada had adopted our version of the Psalter. Or maybe, it's that the congregations simply take pleasure in our psalms and do not observe any special degradation having been inflicted on the older texts. Maybe, they rather observe a later version of Coverdale's work by a distant and admiring cousin having been developed and created with its own vernacular treatment—as a sort of generous and up-to-date homage to the sixteenth-century Reformationist and poetic benefactor.

As I have noted, most scholars agree that the original psalms were composed around 2,500–3,000 years ago, mainly in northern Israel. Considerable speculation exists that one of the oldest is Psalm 89, relying on its references to David as a virtually contemporaneous figure. There is reason to believe that psalmody composition, as reflected in the Psalter, lasted from the Hebraic monarchical period, beginning approximately with David and continuing to near the end of the Old Testament period. Compiled after the Babylonian exile for the second temple, which was, according to several sources, completed toward the end of the sixth century BCE, the Psalter then became part of the temple's worship services. Professor Bernhard W. Anderson wrote that Psalm 119—the so-called Psalter inside the Psalter because of its length—was probably written in this post-exilic period.[2] By that time, the spiritedness of earlier psalms had faded into legalistic pronouncements, as illustrated by Psalm 119. For purposes of dating the beginning and the end, Psalms 89 and 119 are often thought of as good examples of early and late psalmody composition. However, I've concluded that no one knows when the psalms were actually written. We can only approximate by context.

If one were even modestly familiar with the entirety of the Psalter, it is obvious a considerable mixture of tone, purpose, quality, and size exists among the one hundred and fifty poems. Since we've just touched on Psalm 119, a commentary can be applied toward an examination of the miscellany that characterizes the poems of the Psalter. For example, a quick glance at the array of the three psalms, 117–119—closely aligned sequentially, but hardly so in style, length, or message—helps to establish the point. I

---

2. Bernhard W. Anderson, *Understanding the Old Testament* (Englewood Cliffs, NJ: Prentice-Hall, 1986), 567.

could not retell the internal retranslation activities for the drafting committee without giving a measure of attention to Psalm 119. Quite honestly, this peculiar poem still remains for me fixed as a notably exceptional psalm that borders on the annoying. But for a small number of vigorous, inspirational, and inventive lines that sustained us while we wound our way through all 176 verses of this rather repetitive piece of poetry, I have no especially favorable recollections of the experience retranslating this psalm. Of course, a limited number of lines from Psalm 119, such as the following, helped to make the process worthwhile:

> Your word is a lantern to my feet
> and a light upon my path. (v105)[3]

Nonetheless, the length of this poem, combined with the recurring nature of thought and "literary" structure, increase the desire of the translator and the reader, no doubt, to reach the poem's end as soon as possible. Outside of less than a half dozen verses of Psalm 119, the singular or plural forms of one of the following eight words appear in every verse of the poem: *commandment, decree, judgment, law, promise, statute, way,* and *word.* Moreover, there is a doubling-down for which two of these words will occasionally emerge in the very same verse for an even more redundant fare. The image of a corporate lawyer, poring over a contract and occupied with a propensity for defined words to appear regularly throughout a text with the very same definition for the same word, can't help but come to mind whenever I encounter Psalm 119. Notwithstanding the criticality of the few redeeming lines and the appearance of crucial historical language, such as that which gave birth to monastic, canonical hours—"Seven times a day do I praise you" (v164a)[4]—I also can't help but question, this time as a poet, the decision by the compilers of the original Psalter some 2,500 years ago to include this poem, especially when it abuts Psalm 118,

---

3. The Book of Common Prayer, 772.
4. Ibid., 777.

which contains only 29 verses but offers, by comparison, a plenitude of extraordinary lines and memorable verses and half-verses,
such as:

> The same stone which the builders rejected
>   has become the chief cornerstone. (v22)[5]

> This is the Lord's doing,
>   and it is marvelous in our eyes.
> On this day the Lord has acted;
>   we will rejoice and be glad in it. (v23–24)[6]

> Blessed is he who comes in the name of the Lord. (v26a)[7]

At the same time, while in the same physical neighborhood,
numerically speaking, a translator could have taken a short trip for
fresh air and completely missed the retranslation session for the
much abbreviated Psalm 117, consisting of its mere two verses in
total:

> Praise the Lord, all you nations;
>   laud him, all you peoples.

> For his loving-kindness toward us is great,
>   and the faithfulness of the Lord endures for ever.
>   Hallelujah![8]

The miscellany among Psalms 117–119 may be extreme, but
this quality for mixture spreads throughout the Psalter and probably accounts for part of the enduring appeal of these poems, taken
as a whole.

For an accurate understanding of the messages we hear in the
psalms, it is essential to put the Psalter in the context of the people: the Israelites at that time whose religious worship was that of

---

5. Ibid., 762.
6. Ibid.
7. Ibid.
8. Ibid., 760.

a community. We, who are children of the post-Reformation era, who often consider individual, if not individualized, beliefs and private concepts of human and divine conduct virtually the only path to salvation, have much less in common with our forebears, some of whom composed the psalms. It is from this contrasting viewpoint that the psalms were first created, that these special poems came into existence: from an historical and spiritual imperative that a divine relationship existed between the Israelites and God, who would remain involved with His people, including intervention, now and then, often through punishment, such as that experienced in the Babylonian exile, for disobedience. Regardless, there existed a continuing faith that God would not abandon the Hebrews as a community.

Upon their return from Babylon, the Hebrews believed they had an obligation to God that consisted of a renewal of faithfulness in a highly dedicated and demonstrative manner, such as the reconstruction of the temple. In connection with this reconstruction, the psalms became a centerpiece of the Hebraic worship,[9] with the Psalter being the "hymnbook of the second Temple."[10] There were various forms and disciplines of worship, including fasting, the offering of a sacrifice on holy days, and a dance that probably involved accompaniment with a psalm. According to Professor Anderson, "In an 'entrance liturgy' (Psalm 24) we read about the command to the gates of Jerusalem to lift up their arches so that Yahweh, the King of Glory (presumably enthroned invisibly on the Ark) may come in."[11]

> Lift up your heads, O gates;
> lift them high, O everlasting doors;
>   and the King of glory shall come in. (v 7)[12]

9. Anderson, *Understanding the Old Testament*, 520.

10. Ibid., 544.

11. Ibid., 560.

12. The Book of Common Prayer, 614.

After the psalms were enlisted by Hebrews for worship service, both Jews and, then later, Christians adapted the psalms to a wide variety of uses. Once, I walked through the 1979 Book of Common Prayer to uncover the various ways in which the Episcopal Church relies on the psalms. I made it up to eighty uses, and there were still more—from noonday prayer to compline to special days to the offertory to ministry to the sick to burial to ordination. You get the idea.

To understand the particularities of the Episcopal Psalter, it is essential to acknowledge that the psalms did not come to the Book of Common Prayer directly from the original Hebrew language; they actually took a quite circuitous route. The peregrination of the "received text" was long and complex, through a series of "tongues," before the psalms came to rest within the 1979 version of the Book of Common Prayer. One of the more intriguing aspects of the retranslation process concerned the degree to which extensive consideration was paid by the committee to underlying translations and retranslations from which the Psalter in the Book of Common Prayer was derived. Our work involved a series of steps—a form of catenation, if you will—tracing the way in which an individual text was linked to or received by one translation or retranslation and then transmuted to a subsequent one, contributing to an anfractuous journey from the original psalms to the retranslated ones.

When Jews began to spread through various parts of the Greek empire, the need for a Greek translation of Hebrew scriptures, including the psalms, became vital. In response, the Septuagint translation of Hebrew texts into Greek, which had its origin in Alexandria, Egypt, a couple centuries before the birth of Christ, was widely accepted and employed by the Hellenistic Jews. The Septuagint received its name from a legend that seventy scholars had worked independently of each other, with every one of them generating a translation of the scriptures that matched the words of the other sixty-nine. The Septuagint additionally served as an authoritative source for early Christians who spoke and read Greek and who thus relied on the Septuagint for comprehending the Old

Testament, including the psalms. However, over time, when Old Latin supplanted Greek as a result of the rise of the Roman Empire, new translations of the scriptures then took hold, and numerous and differing versions of Old Latin texts appeared, including the psalms, creating a chaotic situation for the Church until Pope Damasus, in the fourth century CE, authorized Jerome to bring order to this farrago through a new Latin retranslation, the Vulgate (Common). Apparently, Jerome had originally intended to complete the translation of the psalms directly from the Hebrew. However, many Christians at the time, because of their knowledge of Greek, resisted that notion, thereby leaving Jerome with the necessity of translating the psalms from the Septuagint into Latin instead. As previously described, Miles Coverdale created his own personal effect on this long and complicated textual saga by becoming a principal figure who chose for his main sources the Vulgate and the then current German versions, mainly Luther's Bible of 1524. Each and every one of these influences bore importantly on the Psalter "received" by the Anglican Church and subsequently the Episcopal Church. As Canon Guilbert has written, "Our Psalter, then, stands at several removes from the Hebrew original, and comes to us steeped in centuries of Jewish and Christian worship and interpretation."[13]

The catenation, this linkage of previous text to more recent text (i.e., Hebrew to Septuagint, Septuagint to Old Latin, Old Latin to Jerome, etc.), added greater variation, curiosity, and story that Coverdale, no doubt, visited from his vantage point but could hardly have unraveled in the same, detailed manner that our twentieth-century committee explored.

The psalms then came to the Episcopal Book of Common Prayer, having gone through several prominent versions, enriched by both Jewish and Christian reverence and praise, but the Coverdale retranslation of the sixteenth century still resonates with his unique voice, for the many elements, including systolic arrangements and figurative compositions, which characterized his original

---

13. Guilbert, *The Prayer Book Psalter Revised*, V.

retranslation, have been preserved within the 1979 Episcopal Book of Common Prayer.

In any event, the initial question must be posed: What was the purpose, in the first place, during the twentieth century of an Episcopal retranslation of the Psalter? The answer is pretty straightforward. Significant scholarship had occurred on the psalms over the several centuries following the first Anglican retranslation, and it had altered elements of the previously assumed meaning of the Hebrew, thereby affecting the validity of certain translated words and phrases contained in the work rendered by Coverdale and earlier translators. Moreover, some of the sixteenth-century language had become obsolete and misleading.

In advance of the decision by the Episcopal Church to retranslate the Psalter for its prayer book, the Church's Standing Liturgical Commission looked at many modern versions for possible usage. None proved adequate for the historical and intended practices, including recitation and singing. The preface to *The Prayer Book Psalter Revised* of 1973, which contained the "trial use" psalms discussed earlier, was authored by the Commission and published as an introductory comment to the preliminary edition for the retranslated Psalter to be included in the Book of Common Prayer. It offered this description to explain the purpose of the retranslation:

> It will be at once apparent from an examination of the psalms in this volume that the Commission is not presenting a new version of the Psalter. This is a further revision of that collection which has been part of the Book of Common Prayer since 1549. It is a continuation of the work of revision which was done for the 1928 edition of the Prayer Book when over a thousand changes were introduced—the most thorough attempt up to that time to bring the fruits of modern biblical scholarship to bear on the Prayer Book Psalter.[14]

---

14. Ibid., II.

A further refinement in applying a more modern approach to the Psalter retranslation was also put in place, including a set of major principles and procedures to be practiced during the retranslation:

1. The psalm text in the prayer book would be revised where a word or passage was deemed to be a mistranslation.

2. The psalm text would also be revised where a word or phrase had become obsolete.

3. When a revision was agreed upon, the primary reference would be assigned to the received Hebrew text, but "full weight" would be given to the Septuagint and to the Vulgate readings, which also stood behind the English.

4. The contemporary second-person pronoun forms would be used, even when addressing God.

5. "O" in the vocative form and "Oh!" as an exclamation would conform to contemporary usage; however, "O" as cohortative, such as "O come let us worship," having fallen entirely into desuetude, would be regarded as obsolete.

6. A decision was made to follow the practice of printing "Lord" in capitals when rendering the divine name *Yahweh* (or *Jehovah*) and "Lord" when translating the word *Adonai*.

7. The Hebrew form of "Hallelujah" was also reinstated, while the Latin form of "Alleluia" and the English equivalent, "Praise the Lord," were excluded.

8. The psalms are a group of ancient poems, but many translations print them simply as prose. The drafting committee decided to print the Psalter as poetry.

9. Finally, one feature of the Episcopal version that doesn't get a lot of attention is the gender neutrality we attempted to achieve—to the extent the original language did not limit the specific meaning to gender case, the drafting committee chose more neutral language.

Bringing these principles down to practice, a few relevant examples have been developed to demonstrate the more noticeable results. Notwithstanding the more than a thousand changes that were made as part of the previous retranslation efforts for the 1928 Psalter, it should be noted that the 1928 edition maintained the Coverdale retranslation even much more intentionally and extensively than the 1979 version. To this point, the examples against which the 1979 Psalter will be compared are from the 1928 version and the psalms contained in Coverdale's 1540 Great Bible.

For obsolete language, I chose Psalm 68:6b. Both the 1928 version and the 1540 Great Bible read: "But letteth the runagates continue in scarceness." This rendition may be effective by being mysterious, but I don't think many people know what runagates are, and, of course, "letteth" had to be adjusted as obsolete. The 1979 version reads: "but the rebels shall live in dry places."

For Psalm 101:5a, the 1928 version and the 1540 Great Bible read: "Whoso privily slandereth his neighbor, him will I destroy." The verb structure, as well as "whoso" and "privily," required change. So, the 1979 version reads: "Those who in secret slander their neighbors I will destroy."

For Psalm 75:6a, the 1928 language and the 1540 Great Bible read: "For promotion cometh neither from the east, nor from the west." The word "promotion" is not the same as "judgment" and needed to be altered. We retranslated the line as: "For judgment is neither from the east nor from the west."

The least controversial of the changes appears to be the adjustment we made to the second-person pronoun, though, in some ways, the removal of the antique words does affect the majesty of the line. For Psalm 9:1, the 1928 prayer book and the 1540 Great Bible read: "I will give thanks unto thee, O Lord, with my whole heart; I will speak of all thy marvelous works." The 1979 reads: "I will give thanks to you, O Lord, with my whole heart; I will tell of all your marvelous works."

As indicated, we eliminated "O" as a cohortative form; the use of an "O" in front of the verb predicate just isn't done any more. Note the line in Psalm 100:3a from both the 1928 prayer book and the 1540 Great Bible: "O go your way into his gates with thanks-giving"; the 1979 Psalter language now becomes: "Enter his gates with thanksgiving."

For a general summary of the principal approach taken by the drafting committee in addressing its overall responsibility for the rendering of the psalms, the following statement illustrates the direction that was taken:

> The Drafting Committee's first task was to produce a translation, as accurate as possible, of the Hebrew text, drawing upon the vast store of recent scholarship of Hebrew and cognate languages and with constant reference to the best scholarly editions of the ancient Greek and Latin versions. Where substantive differences from the Prayer Book version appeared, each was considered carefully to determine whether it represented a legitimate variant translation, a translation from the Greek or Latin, or an obvious mis-translation.[15]

Let's turn our focus to the actual process that was enlisted to achieve the envisioned purposes. I've already described some of the steps that were followed, including the use of Canon Guilbert's drafts of the proposed retranslated psalms circulated to committee members in advance of our sessions, which lasted the better part of a week on a roughly semi-annual basis; I've also touched upon the value of the spreadsheet comparisons using recent, credible psalm translations and retranslations. During the course of our sessions, the consequential view of an English biblical scholar of the nineteenth century, Brooke Foss Westcott, toward our aspiration for eliminating the mistakes in Coverdale's psalms while retaining his style resonated constantly as an essential goal: "[A]nd anyone who will compare the Prayer-Book Psalter with the original (Coverdale) will be able to convince himself that the changes which are needed to remove distinct mistakes could be made without injury to its general character."[16]

---

15. Ibid, X.

16. Driver, ed., *The Parallel Psalter*, xli.

Our sessions were habitually informal but intense. We never had enough space; the bigger the room, the better. Books and papers were spread over everything—thick volumes of Hebrew and Masoretic texts, Greek, Latin, English translations on laps, on the floor, on chair seats, overlapping each other's space on the table, and chairs, more often than not, askew. Yes, it was my kind of place, a bathing in words, if you will: each scholar and participant responding to his own discipline, whatever it may be; the creation of a dangerous form of exercise, just making it safely over and around all the books, briefcases, and papers whenever any of us pursued a visit to the restroom.

Without exception, things began and ended with Canon Guilbert, a tall, not thin, man, formidable in thought, genuineness, expression, and size. There was no doubt among the members that he was the heart and soul of the effort, and yet he accomplished it, as chairman, without arrogance or arbitrary rule. Because we labored independently with Guilbert's drafts in advance of each session, the major obstacles and matters to be addressed came to light rather quickly and early in our discussions. We all liked the idea of identifying any critical point or problem regarding the text to be retranslated before we actually dove into a psalm through a line-by-line process for possible adjustment, which could result from either scholarly or poetic reasons. There were times when the committee overrode Guilbert, who would grudgingly submit to the will of the consensus, but not without reciting the reasons for his disagreement, and not without a certain displeased look or mock cough.

Scholarship had the priority up to a point—the composition of the committee attested to that fact. There was an underlying principle that the integrity and authenticity of our psalms might ultimately be judged harshly if the accuracy and potency of the scholarship were perceived as marginal in the final version. A consensus existed that our rendering would not duplicate the principal shortcoming of Coverdale. However, a lofty level for scholarship needed a limitation, for it was simply not an end in itself, and an underlying caveat maintained a preeminent place within the enterprise: scholarship should not constantly occlude the fluidity and quality of the sound nor the acceptance of the language by those in the pews—an acceptance of the psalms that had been enjoyed by generations of congregations. I was there for a reason, but Canon Guilbert also felt the weight of the burden.

It is an oversimplification to say the process progressed at a regular pace, logically and incrementally firm, and always predictable. That is a bit far from the truth. The resolutions were not routinely sequential. Often someone worked on the side during sessions, away from the group, to arrive at an answer for a single item within a line or verse while the rest of the committee rolled forward, ready to return in an instant when the separate but associated work bore fruit—perhaps, in a few minutes, but often appreciably longer. Iterative might be a better adjective for the arc of the continuum to the endeavor: pushing forward toward a consonant solution for both scholarship and poetry.

Approval by the committee, as a whole, had a way of being amorphous—nothing especially formal attached itself to the setting aside of a completed psalm. I liken it to an inference, an often silent affair toward the end: nothing more to be done with it so the psalm went into the hopper for others, outside the committee, to examine. I analogize this final leg for the committee to a sort of jury with no perfunctory votes and Guilbert serving as foreman, inviting all views at the table to be heard and plumbed. For my part, I often offered, at this point, a correction to the verse if it had not already been accepted, and the committee listened with supporting comments or not. Canon Guilbert frequently arbitrated scholarship and poetry, with a devoted attitude toward scholarship, but not a blind, fixated scope for it, and with a healthy imagination that elevation of language could escort accuracy toward something more valuable than an imperial exercise in good scholarship.

Several times I thought we left a psalm unfinished, though the committee as a whole acted otherwise. If I made my case well enough, we returned to that psalm. Shortly, we will consider a few later adjustments that were accomplished after the 1973 version had been issued for "trial use" and as the psalms were finalized into a more refined and better version. The current prayer book Psalter, the one we produced, is certainly not a perfect document, and I still see lines I'd like to amend for poetic purposes, but it's durable, authentic, and permeated with a literary style resonating with Coverdale's own that has borne the psalms for so long.

I often wondered during the sessions and afterwards—after Auden's death and after the completion of the entirety of our work—what Auden's final judgment and response would have been to the Episcopal retranslation of the psalms. In so many ways, the collective ambition of Charles Guilbert and the committee and that of W. H. Auden were not so dissimilar. Both sides agreed that mistranslations in Coverdale had to be remedied and Coverdale's style retained as much as possible even as his mistakes were removed. I suspected Auden's conclusion would have been that we went too far with the corrections. He would have argued, I think, that there were fewer mistakes in Coverdale than the committee ultimately chose to repair. I also suspect a disagreement on his part with the number of words the committee determined to be obsolete, for Auden often practiced resurrecting old, moldy, or musty words, even for his own writing. Yet, in some ways, I think he would have been less displeased with the final outcome than he feared would have been the case at the beginning of the project in which he participated.

Did I enter each week of the retranslation sessions with a preferred text for every line of the psalms being considered? Yes, I certainly did, but I knew my favorites had to be subject to the tests through which the scholars put the text for accurate content. Not surprisingly, my verse preferences had to be habitually revised, for good reason, in the development of the final text.

What we didn't do, as far as I could tell, was prejudge the theology, the mythology, and the determinative message inherent in each psalm studied. There was a manifest priority to keep any bias or prejudgment at bay. The retranslated text spoke for itself, and work on the poetry proceeded apace. Many times, though, no open issues remained discrete, outstanding, or unresolved toward the end for the poetry of an individual psalm, since those issues had already been addressed in conjunction with the scholarship analysis. In fact, toward the end of many psalm examinations, if the poetry hadn't been fully completed, a phrase or a single (but decisive) word could occasionally finalize the process.

It was inevitable that I would ruminate on the methodology Coverdale may have employed in his own retranslation engagements. Certainly, he never had the benefits and complications akin to our committee seeking together the elevated plateau, and yet, we also know that either while involved with William Tyndale or later, when he had, by his side, the Germans with whom to consult and borrow, Coverdale may have experienced a near collaborative enterprise himself as we had in New York; but he, with less effects from auspices and bureaucracy and ultimately with one hand at the pen, was maybe even favored by the separation and singularity.

Before we eventually settled on a psalm, side conversations always occurred to comply with the proper management of "pointing" in the final verse—essential for the suitable role of choirs and congregations in the singing or chanting of our psalms. Appropriate "pointing" could not be dismissed as a criterion for determining whether we had completed our job well. More discussion of the associated singing and chanting, derivative of the integral "pointing," appears shortly.

When I hear recitations of our psalms Sunday after Sunday, I studiously consider whether we committed any infamous miscues. Upon reflection, I don't think any of our revised verses have come back to bite us, unlike some other translations. For example, there's one line in Psalm 50 from a recent version I'm sure the translators have wished, on more than one occasion, to recall. The 1979 Book of Common Prayer contains the line: "I will take no bull-calf from your stalls."[17] Innocent enough. The other version to which I'm referring, which apparently paid less attention to vernacular speech,

---

17. The Book of Common Prayer, 654.

renders the same line: "I will accept no <u>bull</u> from your house." In current, everyday speech, the latter rendition is hardly the meaning.

I'd like to take a moment and discuss the traditional and contemporary practices in utilizing the psalms for their primary worship purposes. In this respect, it is crucial, at this point, to concentrate on the distinctly liturgical importance these poems have had on Judeo-Christian peoples for approximately three millennia. Canon Guilbert explains the value of the Psalter in the following way:

> [I]t is the liturgical hymnal of the people of God, of the Old Covenant first, but also of the New Covenant—the Christian Church. . . . [I]t has been shaped and molded, and its interpretation enriched, by long liturgical use, in temple, synagogue and church, so that it emerges as a body of praise and prayer suited to the varying but recurrent needs and aspirations of the worshiping community.[18]

Even a surface knowledge of the psalms compels an appreciation for the role these numinous poems, these psalms, have played in a worshipful and liturgical sense—for both Jews and Christians—over many centuries, including their importance to Christ, who, on the night of his arrest, according to the Gospels of both Mark and Matthew, sang a hymn, which is believed to have been a psalm, before going to the Mount of Olives and Gethsemane.

The Psalter is not primarily a body of readings that one reads in solitude, though it can be used that way. It is intended for congregational use. At the same time, personal worship, applied either to individually developed formats or to a more prescribed arrangement, such as a daily lectionary, normally incorporates the reading of psalms. The broader issue that the drafting committee had a responsibility to address was the reading and singing of psalms in a public, reverent, and ceremonious setting, which is a regular practice for use of the psalms in the Episcopal Church. This point was explained in the preface to *The Prayer Book Psalter Revised*:

---

18. Guilbert, *The Psalter: A New Version for Public Worship and Private Devotion*, vi–vii.

A version of the psalms for public worship, therefore, must lend itself to congregational singing and reading. Any text, of course, can be set to music and sung by trained choirs; but the Prayer Book Psalter is demonstrably suitable, because of its flexible prose lines and its strongly rhythmical terminal patterns, both to reading and singing, not only by solo voices, but also in unison, antiphonally, and responsively, by a worshiping congregation.[19]

The drafting committee gave much effort and time to both of these aspects (i.e., corporate reading and singing) during its retranslation sessions. We read individual, retranslated lines out loud—occasionally, several times for an individual psalm—to evaluate the capability of each line to accommodate congregational recitation, which can be accomplished either through direct and unison reading, or through a variety of forms for alternation. Though musical compositional features create quite different structural considerations in singing and chanting from those in the reading of psalms, the option for either direct and unison presentation or alternation of voice or voices remains the same. Indeed, special vigilance and scrutiny were given by the committee, often with vigorous participation by the musicologist, to the "pointing" exercise (i.e., establishment of appropriately stressed syllables) of individual psalm lines to confirm the capability of retranslated psalms for corporate singing and chanting, which have roots deeply embedded in the Judeo-Christian tradition. We've already acknowledged there is ample evidence that the singing of the psalms goes back to early Jewish worship services with the Psalter being known as "the hymn book of the Second Temple, collected and edited to meet the liturgical requirements of the Temple liturgy."[20] Further, plainsong, a generic term for the use of a single unaccompanied melodic line, can be traced back to the early Christian era. Today's congregational singing of psalms to plainsong usually relies on a repeated melodic

---

19. Guilbert, *The Prayer Book Psalter Revised*, V–VI.
20. James Litton, ed., *The Plainsong Psalter* (New York: Church Publishing, 1988), VII.

structure that incorporates an antiphon (a musical refrain, the text of which may be, though not always, chosen from the particular psalm itself) that completes the musical idea of the psalm tone. The other structure, also utilized with the psalms, is the Anglican chant, sung in harmony rather than in unison like plainsong. Anglican chant probably developed out of plainsong in the late sixteenth century and early seventeenth century, reflective of more recent musical patterns being practiced at the time. Anglican chant follows a musical pattern that allows one to sing the psalm harmony while giving attention to the "pointed" syllables. Since modern congregations have, in general, not been schooled in the singing of Anglican chant, the form is quite often sung only by choirs.

The language of the 1979 Psalter is much more accessible than the previous versions and makes both reading and singing much easier. Of course, some people miss the prevailing style of the older 1928 prayer book, and I can understand that proposition. I confess I often recite the Lord's Prayer in the old version on Sunday mornings, but I do believe the Psalter revision, which is not so new any longer, serves the gathered congregation best.

The reaction to the revised Psalter over the years once it became part of the 1979 Book of Common Prayer has, in most respects, been favorable. Beyond the approval expressed by congregations and professional musicians throughout the Episcopal Church, there have been other manifestations of its advantages. For example, Lutherans in the United States and Canada adopted the Psalter in the 1979 Episcopal Book of Common Prayer for service and worship—initially in the *Lutheran Book of Worship*[21] and for the subsequent *Evangelical Lutheran Worship*, although the latter enlisted the Episcopal psalms in a different way. While the *Lutheran Book of Worship* adopted our psalms, the *Evangelical Lutheran Worship* used them as "a primary source and foundation . . . for the version of the Psalms that has been prepared for

---

21. *Lutheran Book of Worship* (Minneapolis: Augsburg Publishing House and Philadelphia: Board of Publication, Lutheran Church in America, 1997), 922. Courtesy of Augsburg Fortress, Publishers.

Evangelical Lutheran Worship,"[22] meaning that the later Lutheran version included adjustments to the Episcopal Psalter.

The Anglican Church of Canada also adopted the Episcopal Psalter for its services and worship in the *Book of Alternative Services*, which, according to the Church's website, has become the "primary worship text for Sunday services and other major liturgical celebrations of the Anglican Church of Canada."[23] One feature of the 1979 retranslated Psalter that needs, at this point, further elaboration regarding its adoption by the Anglican Church of Canada, consists of the drafting committee's attempt at gender neutrality. Canon Guilbert described our approach as follows:

> The psalmists were given to the use of "man" and "children (or sons) of men," and similar terms, where, from the contexts, it is quite clear that those referred to were neither exclusively masculine in gender or singular in number. Some of the passages deal with our common humanity, others are plainly collectives, still others are speaking of our human mortality.[24]

The drafting committee attempted to achieve gender neutrality, as the text allowed, for the attainment of this goal. Set forth below is the commentary by the Anglican Church of Canada regarding the selection of the Episcopal Psalter for its *Book of Alternative Services*, including a few remarks about gender-inclusive language. It should be noted that the Lutherans in the United States and Canada did not provide a similar, expanded expression of rationale in their own book of worship and services for the adoption of the Episcopal Psalter.

> The Psalter which appears in the Book of Common Prayer of the Episcopal Church (U.S.A.) has been selected as an appendix to the Book of Alternative Services. It was chosen because of

---

22. *Evangelical Lutheran Worship* (Minneapolis: Augsburg Fortress Publishers, 2006), 892. Courtesy of Augsburg Fortress Publishers.

23. Anglican Church of Canada, *www.anglican.ca/resources/the-book-of-alternative-services/*.

24. Guilbert, *The Psalter: A New Version for Public Worship and Private Devotion*, xiv.

the verbal accuracy of its translation, because the form is familiar and is highly suitable for use with both plainsong and Anglican chant, and because the translators made an earnest (although not always successful) attempt to use gender-inclusive language whenever possible. This is a good translation, recognizably Anglican in flavour.[25]

The Episcopal Psalter was also adopted as the preferred (now, permitted) psalm translation until the Church of England produced its own version, *Common Worship: Services and Prayers for the Church of England*, in 2000. Subsequently, the Church of England issued *Common Worship: Daily Prayer*, which contained the retranslated psalms appearing in the earlier *Common Worship* volume. It would be worthwhile spending a little time on the Psalter included in the Church of England's *Common Worship* to compare, in certain respects, the approach and results of that Psalter with the psalms contained in the 1979 Book of Common Prayer.

In June 2014, I happened to be in London and attended an Anglican service one Sunday morning. To my surprise, the church I attended had printed in its worship bulletin a portion of Psalm 68 as it appears in our Episcopal Psalter. The occasion piqued my curiosity regarding the connection between the Psalter and those psalms contained in the Church of England's *Common Worship*. To that end, I soon thereafter reached out to the Rt. Rev. David Stancliffe, who held the position of chairman of the Church of England's Liturgical Commission from 1993–2005, during which time both *Common Worship: Services and Prayers for the Church of England* and *Common Worship: Daily Prayer* were first developed, and who is acknowledged as a chief architect of the revised version of the psalms for the Church of England embodied in those two volumes. In August 2014, I prepared a couple of questions for Dr. Stancliffe for the purpose of clarifying the context in which the Church of England employed our Psalter in connection with both the Church of England's liturgy and the preparation of its own psalms included in *Common Worship*. Set forth below are both the specific questions I posed to Dr. Stancliffe and his responses:

1. *To what extent are priests currently at liberty in England to use the American version (Episcopal Psalter)?*

   "One of the things that the Church of England's Liturgical Commission had to do was consider what to do about the Psalter translation when the time came to produce what was to be called *Common Worship* in the 1990s. So we set about exploring alternatives. We certainly considered the Episcopal Psalter, and I had experience with it both in the United States and in certain religious communities in this country, which had used it in preference to any other. This had led to the adoption of your Psalter as the preferred psalm translation in *Celebrating Common Prayer*, the pioneer in reforming the structure and style of the Daily Office, and there is no doubt that many of those in the Liturgical Commission who had been saying the office for a decade using the Episcopal Psalter must have been influenced by it deep down.

   "As we didn't wish to exclude deliberately the continuing use of *Celebrating Common Prayer* for those who had begun to form deep patterns of prayer and had been using it for a good while when we published *Common Worship: Daily Prayer* in 2005, we permitted any version of the Psalter to be used, although by this time we had made our own."

2. *In your work for the* Common Worship *psalms, to what extent, if any, did you refer to/rely upon the Episcopal Psalter?*

   "We did our best to translate the Hebrew first, but had open on the table a plethora of versions: Coverdale (and that is in the memory/marbles of people like me who had been organ scholars, where you can't accompany the psalms to Anglican chants unless you know the words by heart!), the Episcopal

Psalter, Frost Mackintosh, Taizé (in French and English), the current Gelineau/French version, the Scottish drafts, the Vulgate (pretty important), the Septuagint, etc., etc. Although I began working on some initial drafts myself, in correspondence with some Hebrew scholars like John Eaton and John Rogerson, the Commission very soon agreed that a small sub-group should be convened which met for several lengthy periods in South Canonry in Salisbury, where we tested not only the spoken rhythms extensively but also the various options for singing—Anglican chant, Gregorian, simple folk chant, and minimal inflexions. So the greatest influences were probably the subliminal ones of what we had absorbed by using ourselves: in my case, Coverdale, Vulgate, Episcopal Psalter, and the contemporary French."[26]

In conjunction with my communications with Dr. Stancliffe, I've spent considerable time reviewing the psalms included in both *Common Worship* volumes, and I found several major distinctions between the Episcopal Psalter and the *Common Worship* psalms. The obvious differences result from the prevailing principles that drove the respective retranslations. Beyond the desire to translate Hebrew accurately, which was a shared goal for both groups, the drafting committee for the Episcopal Psalter, as mentioned previously, resolved early on to follow a series of guidelines, which have been discussed, such as the elimination of obsolete words and phrases and the cohortative "O" in predicate structures, among other tenets. However, a number of these procedures were not applied to the Church of England version, certainly not in the manner we relied upon them. In addition, the ways in which the two drafting committees conducted the examination of "received text," taking into account any mistranslations from the Hebrew to the Septuagint, the Septuagint to Old Latin, Old Latin to Jerome's Latin, and Jerome's Latin to Coverdale, could render dissimilar

26. E-mail to J. Chester Johnson from the Rt. Rev. David Stancliffe, dated October 13, 2014.

results, especially in the retention or laying aside of various parts of the Coverdale version. The Episcopal Psalter has been praised for its recitation qualities, and by numerous musicians for its singability. Although there are essential differences between the two Psalter versions, there is little doubt that the two shared these requisite goals in the preparation of their respective Psalters.

Over the period of the Episcopal retranslation project, extending from 1967 until publication of the 1979 Book of Common Prayer, four official documents were made public, illuminating and illustrating the important phases and germane aspects of the Psalter retranslation. Three years following authorization of prayer book revision—of which the Psalter was a part—by the General Convention, the Episcopal Church's governing body, the Standing Liturgical Commission issued in 1970 a volume entitled *The Psalter, Part I, A Selection of the Most Frequently Appointed Psalms, Prayer Book Studies 23*. The document presented for the first time to the public and the Episcopal community a sampling of the drafting committee's continuing work and an overview of its approach and principles. This volume of nearly 120 pages introduced a collection of the most frequently used psalms. In addition, it listed the names of the eight members (one of whom had resigned in 1969) for the then drafting committee, including Canon Guilbert, W. H. Auden, and Professor Robert C. Dentan. The interim publication also recited several of the basic procedures for and intrinsic background on the Psalter program, such as:

1. The new version would be "a further revision of that Psalter which has been a part of the Book of Common Prayer (with very little change) since 1549. . . ."

2. The reasons, peculiar and patent to Episcopalians, for not adopting any of the other recent psalm translations.

3. The history and use of the Psalter that has been continued in numerous prayer books since the 1549 original.

4. The salient guidelines of the drafting committee that would be repeated to the completion of the retranslation, including the

elimination of mistranslations, obsolete words and phrases, and cohortative predicate structures; use of the contemporary second-person form, even when addressing God; and presentation formats.

5. The anticipated employment of the retranslated psalms for choir and congregational singing and chanting and for congregational recitation.

6. An explanation of verse breaks and the extensive historical reliance by the Prayer Book Psalter on varied constructs of the classical "cursus" system of Latin accentual prose rhythm before strong pauses; it emphasizes that the prayer book Psalter has contained a higher proportion of these rhythmic patterns than the King James Bible and a much higher proportion than ordinary prose.[27]

Subsequent volumes, both interim and final, on the committee's work return to most of these descriptions of underlying tenets and historical characteristics that affected much of the process and results reflected in the retranslated psalms.

Approximately three years later, the Standing Liturgical Commission issued a subsequent interim document for "trial use." The volume was entitled *The Prayer Book Psalter Revised* and contained drafts of the entire body of the one hundred and fifty psalms with revision to a number of those that had been embodied within *The Psalter, Part I, A Selection of the Most Frequently Appointed Psalms, Prayer Book Studies 23*. It would be incorrect to assume that the second interim volume, while containing all of the Psalter, ended the work of the drafting committee; one need only compare these psalms with the final version of the Psalter that is part of the 1979 Book of Common Prayer to recognize that many changes ensued between the 1973 interim psalms for the entire Psalter and the rendering of the psalms as they ultimately appeared in the 1979

---

27. Standing Liturgical Commission of the Episcopal Church, *The Psalter, Part I, A Selection of the Most Frequently Appointed Psalms, Prayer Book Studies 23* (New York: The Church Hymnal Corporation, 1970), 1–13.

prayer book. We will shortly review a few examples of the adjustments that transpired in language for certain key lines after the publication of the 1973 *Prayer Book Psalter Revised*.

The 1973 volume retained much of the introductory discussion that had been part of *The Psalter, Part I, A Selection of the Most Frequently Appointed Psalms, Prayer Book Studies 23*; however, a few amendments and additions were included:

1. The Psalter retranslation represents "a continuation of the work of revision which was done for the 1928 edition of the Prayer Book. . . ."

2. The Coverdale Psalter "antedates the King James Version by three-quarters of a century, and its version of the psalms had so commended itself to Churchmen that when the decision was made to adopt the King James Version for Epistles and Gospels, which happened in 1662, the older translation of the psalms was retained. . . ."

3. The suggestion was rejected that "some of the psalms, or portions of the psalms, be omitted, as being unsuited to Christian devotion."

4. The introduction also explains the roots of Christian worship being bound in the psalms, demonstrated by psalmody's role in the Eucharistic service; the introduction also describes the way the psalms have played an essential role in regular and congregational recitation and in monastic and individual formats for the daily office and the lectionary.

5. The "caesura," or dividing point for psalm verses, was explained, indicating that such breakage would be illustrated in the prayer book by "the caesura with a symbol." Actually, the Psalter within the 1979 Book of Common Prayer retained, for this purpose, the use of an asterisk for verse division, which had also been the practice for the 1928 Book of Common Prayer.[28]

---

28. Guilbert, *The Prayer Book Psalter Revised*, I–XII.

Reference was also made to the membership at that time of the drafting committee, a subject that has already been examined. *The Prayer Book Psalter Revised* became the final interim publication for "trial use."

In 1978, one year before our retranslated Psalter appeared in the revised Episcopal Book of Common Prayer, a volume entitled *The Psalter, A New Version for Public Worship and Private Devotion*, authored by Canon Guilbert and distributed by Seabury Press, the then publishing arm of the Episcopal Church, became available to interested persons, both Episcopalian and those outside the Church's corporate body. Guilbert included our completed, retranslated Psalter and a much expanded explanatory introduction on the psalms, as the drafting committee had addressed them, and on a series of associated subjects, pertinent to the version that had been produced. He also altered remarks he made in the explicative material placed in the 1970 and 1973 presentations. For example, Guilbert previously stated in both documents that the Psalter of the Book of Common Prayer "derives from the Great Bible of 1536" of Miles Coverdale, but, in fact, Coverdale made manifold adjustments to those psalms of the earlier bible, and it is rather his later bible of 1540 on which the Psalter of the Book of Common Prayer relies most heavily.

Further, Canon Guilbert gives appreciable space in the 1978 introduction to the sundry forms of the parallelism embodied in the poetry of the psalms. From the "symmetry of sense" that establishes the foundation for this parallelism, Guilbert proceeds to describe the main types of parallelism that "were identified by Bishop Robert Lowth of England in the eighteenth century," for which examples are presented below:

1. Synonymous:

   Lord, who may dwell in your tabernacle?
      who may abide upon your holy hill? (Psalm 15:1)

2. Antithetical:

   For the Lord knows the way of the righteous,
      but the way of the wicked is doomed. (Psalm 1:6)

3. Synthetic (e.g., relation of cause and effect):

Those who are planted in the house of the Lord
   shall flourish in the courts of our God. (Psalm 92:12)

4. Synthetic (e.g., relation of condition and result):

If I forget you, O Jerusalem,
   let my right hand forget its skill. (Psalm 137:5)[29]

Certain other areas of primary importance engage Guilbert's attention in the enhanced introduction. He discloses the methodology of the committee to arrive at more gender-neutral language—with emphasis on the opportunities permitted. Additionally, he goes into considerable length to recite the suitable classifications of the Psalter, from hymns of praise to lamentations to imprecatory and pilgrim psalms, among others. Of definite note is Guilbert's discussion of the role of the psalms in Christianity. Though the psalms are Hebraic in origin, there can be no doubt that they settled into a very special role for the Christian, as seen when one practices a little exegesis on the New Testament and its multitude of references to the psalms. Guilbert poses, in effect, a dialectic between the proposition that the psalms are messianic in their nature versus a proposition that the psalms be understood "entirely in terms of their own times and situations."[30] Personally, I don't perceive an irreconcilable dilemma at all with these two theses when they are conveyed through elemental time, for both prognosis and hindsight are equally captured by the psalms, often in identical words and phrases.

In the following year, our retranslated Psalter was made part of the revised Book of Common Prayer. Various sections or concepts set forth in the explanatory introductions for the three previous documents published in 1970 (*The Psalter, Part I, A Selection of the Most Frequently Appointed Psalms, Prayer Book Studies 23*), 1973 (*The Prayer Book Psalter Revised*), and 1978 (*The Psalter, A New Version for Public Worship and Private Devotion*), respectively, were

---

29. Guilbert, *The Psalter: A New Version for Public Worship and Private Devotion*, vii–viii.
30. Ibid., xxiii–xxiv.

inserted in the new prayer book for a little more than two pages, as a brief, separate piece called "Concerning the Psalter." Principal areas explored in that piece are: the nominal terms used with reference to God in the new retranslation; the four traditional methods for psalm recitation among congregations; and the forms of the poetic device, parallelism, found in the psalms.[31]

Within an earlier discussion, I commented on the work that had been accomplished by the drafting committee between 1973 and the Psalter published in the 1979 Book of Common Prayer to improve the fluidity and poetic language of the 1973 "trial use" version. The following compares only a sampling of single lines—a few stark examples of the phraseology of the final revised Psalter with that which had been published earlier; the reader can receive a flavor of the alteration in approach to the language of poetry that occurred between the two versions:

Psalm 33:19b
1973: and to keep them in the time of dearth.
1979: and to feed them in time of famine.

Psalm 34:6a
1973: This afflicted one called, and the Lord heard
1979: I called in my affliction and the Lord heard me

Psalm 78:4a
1973: the praise-worthy deeds of the Lord, and his power,
1979: the praiseworthy deeds and the power of the Lord,

Psalm 84:10a
1973: For the Lord God is a sun and a shield;
1979: For the Lord God is both sun and shield;

Psalm 86:15a
1973: But you, O Lord, are compassionate and gracious,
1979: But you, O Lord, are gracious and full of compassion,

---

31. The Book of Common Prayer, 582–84.

Psalm 88:4b

1973: I have become like a man with no strength left;
1979: I have become like one who has no strength;

Psalm 105:13b

1973: and from one kingdom to another people,
1979: and from one kingdom to another,

Psalm 147:10a

1973: He provides food for the cattle
1979: He provides food for flocks and herds

During the time frame from 1973 to final publication, a multiplicity of adjustments were made to the Psalter. It may come as a shock that we exercised a few style changes to Coverdale's words and lines during this period, even when such changes did not fit neatly into the main guidelines established for the committee. In an instance shown above, we deleted the Coverdale word "people" at the end of the line in Psalm 105:13b for simply being surplus, as "people" imparted no relevant meaning and damaged the poetry. The line accordingly reads much better. I could also point out other examples where the editing away of Coverdale for similar reasons became a recognized obligation and service. Of course, I failed to convince in many battles over the poetry (probably, on frequent occasions, to the betterment of the document), though I think the committee reacted favorably more often than not. Even so, when I read over the final Psalter, I'm disappointed some of my proposals didn't succeed. For example:

Psalm 95:6a

1979 Psalter: Come, let us bow down, and bend the knee,
My Choice: Come, let us worship and bow down,

Psalm 140:4b

1979 Psalter: who are determined to trip me up.
My Choice: who plot my downfall.

Also, for Psalm 109:20a, we had applied the exclamation "oh," which was permitted under our guidelines, but it had taken the form of a cohortative in this peculiar case, as in "oh, deal with me according to your Name;" which was not allowed, so I would have eliminated the construct altogether and adopted the more straight-forward: "deal with me according to your Name," but alas, the suggestion did not carry the day. The accepted language in that verse still seems to bear an oddness to it. Although these random samples demonstrate a failure to persuade, I received my fair share of textual recommendations that were subsequently made part of the final version.

That I lived longer than most members of the committee means I had a much more extended period of time to hear and read our psalms over and over again throughout the years, both in church and at home, so the prospect of what could have been has resonated a very long time—long enough for me to revisit the consequences of our Psalter, to relish more than to re-judge our decisions, which, on the whole, I've concluded, were the right ones time and time again. While there were scant moments of disap-pointment over certain pieces of resultant text and over the ram-ification of utterances from one or two members who displayed a different ear (from mine, at least), these sharply unfamiliar intervals rapidly dissipated in the face of the habitual goodwill and constant intelligent and quite memorable contributions that members of the committee routinely offered toward the ultimate re-creation of a remarkable, lucid, and fulgent Psalter for the Episcopal Church and, to my later amazement and delight, for Lutherans in the United States and Canada and for many fellow Anglicans in Canada and England.

CHAPTER 9

∽

Psalms in the Balance

OR MANY OF US, there is a certain irreducible and personal history, extracted and carried discretely and convincingly by the psalms—a familiar voice and a phrase or verse to follow, or a phrase or verse and the distilled instant returns. This chapter invites a remembrance of things, fates, once sheltered by time, but once named, they are disclosed, even occasionally feared. These psalms in the balance: pended, suspended, but still more than real. For in the balance, they become vivid, primitive, visceral.

It has been postulated several times in this volume that the drafting committee for the retranslation of the psalms in the late 1960s and 1970s followed the principle that the stylistic qualities and adroit facility contained in the Psalter of Miles Coverdale should be significantly maintained within the committee's retranslation for inclusion in the 1979 Book of Common Prayer. This chapter will confirm, through the retranslation engendered, the committee's adherence to this guideline. Suspicions by W. H. Auden to the contrary notwithstanding, which a few observers have, over the years, characterized as being an accurate assessment of the drafting committee's true aspirations, the noted liturgist and professor Marion J. Hatchett, author of *Commentary on the American Prayer Book*, concluded nearly two decades after the 1979 Book of Common Prayer was published that the final text of the revised Episcopal Psalter established a definite connection with the past and more particularly with Coverdale's psalms: ". . . the vocabulary of the revised version of the Psalter is limited for the most part to that used by Coverdale in the sixteenth century."[1] This connection to Coverdale's psalms in the work by and goals of the drafting committee had often been unacknowledged and unanticipated by many of those interested in the Psalter revision project, including, if not especially, W. H. Auden. In this chapter, I will show a comparison between Coverdale's psalms, updated with more recognizable and modernized spelling and punctuation, and the Psalter contained in the 1979 Book of Common Prayer. The comparison will demonstrate the conspicuous linkage in style and word selection between the two versions—illustrating the heavy reliance the most recent Episcopal Psalter placed on Coverdale's retranslation, though this 1979 version, which adheres to a set of guidelines that incorporated more modern scholarship, language procedures, and techniques, is less fully dependent on Coverdale than the preceding 1928 Episcopal Psalter.

So, how to integrate the style characteristics found of Coverdale into the drafting committee's retranslation project? First, we kept adjustments to his former language and word order (for rhythmic retention purposes) to a minimum. Second, we maintained, to the maximum extent possible, the discipline that changes to Coverdale would necessarily and principally result from obsolete words and mistranslations. Of course, mistranslations created special problems for the committee, as they might not be restricted to a single word in a phrase or clause. Rather, the more severe problem occurs when a mistranslation applies to an entire phrase or clause; at these times, the committee either attempted to duplicate with entirely new language a structure similar to the one utilized by Coverdale, or generated an ad hoc phrase or clause that linked well with the existing language of the line. It is easy to understand then that the duplication of structure and the development of an entirely new ad hoc phrase or clause, both actions of which are to be "in the spirit" of Coverdale, constitute a challenging feat. Actually, I think those attempts represent the situs for most criticism that has, on occasion, been aimed at the committee's output.

---

1. Marion J. Hatchett, *Commentary on the American Prayer Book* (New York: HarperCollins, 1995), 28.

Laced within the following contents of this chapter will be found a sampling of select psalms, each presented in two versions: one fashioned by Coverdale for the 1540 Great Bible and the other contained in the 1979 Book of Common Prayer. The reader will be able to judge the extent to which the 1979 Psalter bears a similarity to Coverdale's psalms—more particularly, "in the spirit" of Coverdale. It can be a tricky business to follow in a decidedly deliberate way the work of another, especially when over four hundred years have elapsed since the contrasted work was published. Nevertheless, considering the guidelines followed by the drafting committee, combined with the age difference between the two retranslations, it is somewhat remarkable that numerous telltale qualities stand out in the 1979 Episcopal Psalter that draw directly and distinctly from the earlier, sixteenth-century one.

In comparing the two retranslations below, one will discover that there are individual lines between the two that have been retranslated in an identical manner or with only modest adjustments, reflecting, in the Episcopal psalms, more modern conventions of language and form. Additionally, a reader can note quite similar devices exhibited in the two retranslations for pivoting from an entire poem line to a subsequent one or from one full verse to a following one. The running of the new line routinely, though not always, carries a related weight and sense to the earlier sixteenth-century rendition. Of course, there would admittedly be an inability for the 1979 Episcopal Psalter to duplicate the antiquity and the associated force of some of the Coverdale language that make it special to many without our violating principles that guided the drafting committee (i.e., "promotion" does not mean "judgment," and "runagates" is meaningless to the contemporary ear). That being said, some would argue such antiquation has a poetic effect that can't be replicated through current expressions. Frankly, however, a fascination with the use and repetition of truly antique words and expressions for their sake—there could be consequential damage to communication and clarity by such use and repetition—extended well beyond the responsibilities and mandate of our committee.

While our retranslation could approximate the running of Coverdale lines, there were syllabic and correlative accentual compromises that were necessary with the text we inherited. For example, Coverdale chose to employ the two-syllable word "whither" from time to time; our age's equivalent is the monosyllabic word "where." Such examples have only modest impacts for establishing shades of difference in a line, but were necessary. Indeed, it is especially critical to note that the more often obsolete words and mistranslations happened in the Coverdale text, the greater distance our retranslation migrated away from his language.

As a youngster, I had my first substantive exposure to the psalms through memorization and recitation in a public setting at the local Methodist church I attended from first grade until I graduated from high school. Early on in grade school, several of us were expected to memorize certain psalms and then stand before the congregation and deliver them flawlessly. Inasmuch as school and church had not yet become separable, in any practical sense, in that part of the country, we often had an obligation to undergo a similar drill at school. In fact, because my fifth grade teacher at school had also been my Sunday school teacher, I would frequently get excused from class work at the public school to go into an unused classroom to practice the delivery of an individual psalm for an upcoming worship service where the entire congregation of the First United Methodist Church in Monticello, Arkansas, could hear my recitation. I wouldn't dare make a mistake with family, friends of family, and teachers sitting in the congregation attentively and listening to every intonation and accented syllable. And certainly, no written or shorthand notes were allowed. I can still remember waking in the middle of the night and mentally practicing lines of the psalms to be delivered.

One could easily confer on that experience the likely prospect for an adult aversion to the psalms, but it had the direct opposite effect. I came to recall, without even thinking about it, the cadence, the repeated sounds of the words strung together. During those earlier, tender years, I didn't understand the meaning very well, but the King James language, which had relied on Coverdale's Psalter by making only "slight alterations" to his retranslation,[2] stayed in my memory vaults and became quite natural and easy to reclaim from time to time, like index cards stored for a research project. I don't think the rhythm of the psalms has ever fully left me, from those days when I stood in front of an assembly of whole families, when I felt those people were likely the whole universe, the stars and galaxies, the Milky Way—in some ways, God Himself, hearing how I measured, timed, elocuted the lines of his psalms.

Only later did the substance make its entrance. I fought off the meaning of the words for years until it wasn't sensible to do so any longer. I know the fascination with the history of those verses came first before the exegesis, imagining a David there in composition with his lyre or harp, chanting out the words, empowering the precise Hebrew words on the way to the creation of a poem.

There are multiple ways to frame the psalms, and scholars and writers have chosen an assortment of approaches over the years. For me, it makes the most sense to look at them with an eye toward six categorizations: royalty, supplication, lamentation, adoration, imprecation, and humanism. I'm most attracted to the humanist psalms: examples of this literary style or approach are Psalms 23, 137, and 139, among others—genuine human efforts and searches amid doubt, uncertainties, desperation, belief, consolations, weakness, and strength. Psalm 139:6–9 serves as an illustration:

Coverdale's 1540 Great Bible Psalter:

Whither shall I go then from thy Spirit,
  or whither shall I go then from thy presence?
If I climb up into heaven, thou art there;
  if I go down to hell, thou art there also.
If I take the wings of the morning
  and remain in the uttermost parts of the sea,
Even there also shall thy hand lead me
  and thy right hand shall hold me.

---

2. Nicolson, *God's Secretaries*, 249.

1979 Episcopal Psalter:

Where can I go then from your Spirit?
    where can I flee from your presence?
If I climb up to heaven, you are there;
    if I make the grave my bed, you are there also.
If I take the wings of the morning
    and dwell in the uttermost parts of the sea,
Even there your hand will lead me
    and your right hand hold me fast.

Of course, there is adoration here, but underlying that adoration are the manifest desperation and poignancy that accompany the simple act of living every day: a magnificent reach forward to a magnificent something beyond, encompassing and holding life unbroken, if not elusively. The effect of a mysterious presence of danger ("And dwell in the uttermost parts of the sea") sets a reason for the hand that does not deny nor forsake. The poem, the psalm, as evidenced by these lines alone, creates an energy of passion that bears the human state and then suspends all in anticipation of ultimate safety, correction, if you will, and salvation.

These lines of poetry from the humanistic Psalm 139 strike a special, personal chord. A friend and classmate of mine at Harvard, who also hailed from Arkansas, encountered an especially rough several years emotionally and psychologically from his late teens until he died in his early twenties from hepatitis. He never knew his father, who had served in the U.S. Air Force during World War II as a fighter pilot and who was lost at sea in the Pacific Theater. After my friend's death, the family decided—quite eloquently, I thought—to bury him beside his father, whose tombstone carried lines of poetry cited above from Psalm 139, and to have those very same lines of poetry also appear on my friend's tombstone.

From the close and intimate, I'd like to move to the geographically remote, but nonetheless humanistically potent: the Babylonian exile by the ancient Hebrews, described in Psalm 137:1–4.

Coverdale's 1540 Great Bible Psalter:

By the waters of Babylon we sat down and wept,
    when we remembered thee, O Sion.
As for our harps, we hanged them up,
    upon the trees that are therein.
For they that led us away captive required of us then a song
and melody in our heaviness:
    "Sing us one of the songs of Sion."
How shall we sing the Lord's song
    in a strange land?

1979 Episcopal Psalter:

By the waters of Babylon we sat down and wept,
    when we remembered you, O Zion.
As for our harps, we hung them up
    on the trees in the midst of that land.
For those who led us away captive asked us for a song,
and our oppressors called for mirth:
    "Sing us one of the songs of Zion."
How shall we sing the Lord's song
    upon an alien soil?

The above excerpt from Psalm 137 tells a graphic 2,600-year-old story of a forced march across an ancient world. With the Israelites exiled, enslaved, having endured a coffle from Jerusalem and Judah to Babylon upon the sacking of their native land and the blinding of their king Zedekiah by Nebuchadnezzar in 587 BCE, it is easy to imagine the degradation and despondency gripping the poet writing these lines, provoked to perform a psalm or similar song for the conquering army, conveying these Israelites to a foreign place and to a completely unknown, servile, and subordinate life. These psalms, songs of sanctity when sung in Judah, are demeaned to be sung for mere entertainment and likely ridicule by the nonbeliever. Nearer to home, one can conjure the effects on the six Indian nations directed through the unlawful and forced trek of the Trail of Tears during the 1830s, from the rich lands of the American Southeast, along western and northwestern routes, and pushed for continual movement through snow, rain, starvation, disease, and death. Large percentages of those coerced to make the long marches perished on the way that followed a path, not far from the place of my youth, through Arkansas. "How shall we sing . . . upon an alien soil?"

One cannot know much about the march from Jerusalem to Babylon in 587 BCE, but for the murderous, vengeful attitude of the Hebrew poet of Psalm 137, as illuminated by the poem's last two verses (8–9):

Coverdale's 1540 Great Bible Psalter:

O daughter of Babylon, wasted with misery;
    yea, happy shall he be that rewardeth thee
    as thou hast served us.
Blessed shall he be that taketh thy children,
    and throweth them against the stones.

1979 Episcopal Psalter:

O Daughter of Babylon, doomed to destruction,
    happy the one who pays you back
    for what you have done to us!
Happy shall he be who takes your little ones,
    and dashes them against the rock!

Was it as bad as the American Trail of Tears? Or the death run from the Buna camp at Auschwitz to Gleiwitz and then by train, in open-air cattle and freight cars, during the winter of January 1945, to Buchenwald, as told by Elie Wiesel in *Night*? Of the one hundred persons who had started by train in Wiesel's open-air car from Gleiwitz, Poland, only twelve remained alive when the slow train, after days and nights traveling through ever-falling snow and relentlessly freezing temperatures, finally arrived, four hundred miles later, at Buchenwald.[3]

Looking back, looking homeward, I believe it must have been Psalm 23, especially verses 1–4, that first embedded itself as inescapable, recollected poetry of the psalms:

Coverdale's 1540 Great Bible Psalter:

The Lord is my shepherd;
  therefore can I lack nothing.
He shall feed me in a green pasture
  and lead me forth beside the waters of comfort.
He shall convert my soul
  and bring me forth in the paths of righteousness for his Name's sake.
Yea, though I walk through the valley of the shadow of death,
I will fear no evil,
  for thou art with me;
  thy rod and thy staff comfort me.

1979 Episcopal Psalter:

The Lord is my shepherd;
  I shall not be in want.
He makes me lie down in green pastures
  and leads me beside still waters.
He revives my soul
  and guides me along right pathways for his Name's sake.
Though I walk through the valley of the shadow of death,
I shall fear no evil;
  for you are with me;
  your rod and your staff, they comfort me.

In this case, it had less to do with the local Methodist church and more to do with my paternal family, who lived only three

---

3. Elie Wiesel, *The Night Trilogy* (New York: Hill and Wang, 2008), 121.

blocks away from us and next to the county courthouse. The home stood right across the street from the Methodist church in that small Arkansas town. My father died when I was one, and the dead of the family—more particularly the departed men—had somehow, according to Johnson myth and lore, lived more perfect, conscious, and conscientious lives than all the rest of us who still resided among the breathing. At least, that was the milieu, the codified pulse, the instinctive doctrine elevated by the paternal family. Unfortunately, this attitude, widely known in Monticello, had the unsurprising effect of being seen by a large segment of townsfolk as bordering a bit on hagiography, with the consequence that many of my childhood friends were so scared of the interior of my paternal family's home that, despite my best efforts, they couldn't be persuaded even to enter the house—at least, not until near the end of our high school years. Nonetheless, as I heard or read the first four verses of Psalm 23 early in my life, I could, in fact, imaginatively envision a brave father— my father surely—walking "through the valley of the shadow of death," unafraid.

In Psalm 23, the contrast between danger and assurance, evil and coherence, moves through the poetry with a courage that is unmistakable. The lines from this poem are immortal verses that have given solace and strength to the human community, even to those who may not fully believe in a spiritual essence from a divine presence, who cannot accept divinity in the bleakest of prospects, or in those horrific moments when some might say no God could possibly be present to allow pain and evil to dwell so easily, so comfortably, and seemingly unopposed. It is this convergence of trials weighed against a triumphant assurance, regardless of temporary outcomes, that makes a humanistic poem like Psalm 23 so powerful, relevant, and inviting.

At the same time, multiple verses of Psalm 90 face toward a somewhat obversely different direction, and yet my older brother and I were, when young, also expected to commit certain of its lines to memory. Below is Psalm 90:10–12:

Coverdale's 1540 Great Bible Psalter:

The days of our age are threescore years and ten,
and though men be so strong that they come to fourscore years,
 yet is their strength then but labor and sorrow;
 so soon passeth it away, and we are gone.
But who regardeth the power of thy wrath?
For even thereafter as a man feareth, so is thy displeasure.
O teach us to number our days
 that we may apply our hearts unto wisdom.

1979 Episcopal Psalter:

The span of our life is seventy years,
perhaps in strength even eighty;
 yet the sum of them is but labor and sorrow,
 for they pass away quickly and we are gone.
Who regards the power of your wrath?
 who rightly fears your indignation?
So teach us to number our days
 that we may apply our hearts to wisdom.

When I was a child, my mother unhesitatingly admitted to her demotion of God from a position of importance, although her views about such things changed later in life. It was not that she preferred being an atheist or agnostic, which would have implied an attitude of determined indifference; no, she just disliked God outright and felt unrelieved anger, since she blamed God both for my father's premature demise and for not giving her what she believed should have been at least consolation and comfort at the time of her husband's passing. Mother often expressed this anger as she drove my brother and me the short distance to the Methodist church on Sunday mornings. Nonetheless, she remained insistent we attend Sunday school and church, though she would only infrequently join us for services, usually on those few Sundays one of us performed. Inexplicably, she also instructed us to memorize a prayer our father apparently recited when an occasion required, with the final line being verse twelve of Psalm 90: "So teach us to number our days that we may apply our hearts unto wisdom" (KJV).

The currency of the psalms carried forward into the modern and postmodern world cannot be better demonstrated than through the special adoption—as an often applied mantra—of the cadential two words "How long" from Psalm 13, during the civil rights movement in the United States from 1950–1970. Here are the apropos verses, Psalm 13:1–2:

Coverdale's 1540 Great Bible:

How long wilt thou forget me, O Lord, for ever?
  how long wilt thou hide thy face from me?
How long shall I seek counsel in my soul,
and be so vexed in mine heart?
  How long shall mine enemy triumph over me?

1979 Episcopal Psalter:

How long, O Lord?
will you forget me for ever?
  how long will you hide your face from me?
How long shall I have perplexity in my mind,
and grief in my heart, day after day?
  how long shall my enemy triumph over me?

The appropriation of "how long" as a mantra for the civil rights movement also illustrates the way poetry and reason can coalesce in memory to expound phrases and clauses from the psalms that are both spontaneously genuine and persuasive. It would indeed be hard to convince me that Martin Luther King, Jr., and his associates did not hearken back within their own memory vaults to Psalm 13 as a reference point for the phrase, quoted so often during the civil rights struggle, which depended on the plaintive grievance, measure, and simple pleas that echoed the ancient Israelites' plight in Hebrew poetry to reveal the African-Americans' own calamity, more particularly in the American South, and to appeal for divine protection and deliverance.

To some, the psalms are mere curios—rare, maybe even unique messages—from a remote, antique culture: curious, literary baubles to be valued at a distance in time, condescendingly, perhaps, and accompanied by more than a little sophisticated urbanity. Yet, others seek and secure contemporaneity in Psalter verses, such as Psalm 74:3–7:

Coverdale's 1540 Great Bible Psalter:

Lift up thy feet that thou mayest utterly destroy every enemy,
    which hath done evil in thy sanctuary.
Thine adversaries roar in the midst of thy congregations
    and set up their banners for tokens.
He that hewed timber afore out of the thick trees
    was known to bring it to an excellent work.
But now they break down all the carved work thereof
    with axes and hammers.
They have set fire upon thy holy places
    and have defiled the dwelling-place of thy Name,
      even unto the ground.
Yea, they said in their hearts, "Let us make havoc of them altogether."
    Thus have they burnt up all the houses of God
      in the land.

1979 Episcopal Psalter:

Turn your steps toward the endless ruins;
    the enemy has laid waste everything in your sanctuary.
Your adversaries roared in your holy place;
    they set up their banners as tokens of victory.
They were like men coming up with axes to a grove of trees;
    they broke down all your carved work with hatchets
      and hammers.
They set fire to your holy place;
    they defiled the dwelling-place of your Name
    and razed it to the ground.

They said to themselves, "Let us destroy them altogether."
They burned down all the meeting-places of God
in the land.

Dietrich Bonhoeffer, who was murdered in a Nazi concentration camp, visualized Kristallnacht (Night of Broken Glass), an historic incident of German and Austrian anti-Semitism, through the above lines from the Psalter. Bonhoeffer's principal biographer and closest friend, Eberhard Bethge, suggests Bonhoeffer saw in these verses Nazi soldiers passing before his mind's eye as they roared in their destruction of over a thousand synagogues in Germany and Austria, and as they tore through countless Jewish homes and businesses, promoting savage anti-Semitism in their wake. In the margin of his Bible alongside the relevant verses of Psalm 74, Bonhoeffer had written the date, 9.11.38 (November 9, 1938). In close proximity to the above special verses, he had also effected definite marks with a stroke and an exclamation point.[4] The words crafted 2,500–3,000 years ago painted a news report with a corresponding exegesis given body by the ancient poem, seen in the present for elemental clarity.

Psalm 103 is not emphasized here simply for its poetry, but for its sentiments, its empathy, and its theology, which are exhibited in its verses, 2–8:

Coverdale's 1540 Great Bible Psalter:

Praise the Lord, O my soul,
    and forget not all his benefits,
Which forgiveth all thy sin
    and healeth all thine infirmities;
Which saveth thy life from destruction
    and crowneth thee with mercy and loving kindness;
Which satisfieth thy mouth with good things,
    making thee young and lusty as an eagle.

---

4. Bonhoeffer, *Prayerbook of the Bible*, 148.

The Lord executeth righteousness
    and judgment for all them that are oppressed with wrong.
He showed his ways unto Moses,
    his works unto the children of Israel.
The Lord is full of compassion and mercy,
    long suffering, and of great goodness.

1979 Episcopal Psalter:

Bless the Lord, O my soul,
    and forget not all his benefits.
He forgives all your sins
    and heals all your infirmities;
He redeems your life from the grave
    and crowns you with mercy and loving kindness;
He satisfies you with good things,
    and your youth is renewed like an eagle's.
The Lord executes righteousness
    and judgment for all who are oppressed.
He made his ways known to Moses
    and his works to the children of Israel.
The Lord is full of compassion and mercy,
    slow to anger and of great kindness.

It's well known that the psalms contain the imprecations and elocutions for fire and brimstone here and there among those pages, accenting anguish and vengeance, which cause a fair number of readers to eschew the Psalter all together. And while prospects for terror and punishment of the unfaithful and wicked may not necessarily be suffusive throughout the entirety of the Psalter, they are nonetheless common in the set of imprecatory poems—sometimes harsh and noisy, sometimes violent and resembling, on occasion, Homer's sanguinary battle poetry. In this distinction of verbal mood and expression, we can and should acknowledge that tumult and trauma imply the call and search for a quick finish, while certainty and assuring presence can calmly extend a moment fearlessly

into the unknown, the unknowable and timeless. Therefore, the
countervailing supply of less "fear and trembling" monologues,
lines that invite readers through more mercy and tenderness, can
provide a welcomed, persuasive balm at a time when biblical scripture falls on many deaf ears in the aftermaths of Hiroshima and
the Holocaust, when the question "Where was God?" receives no
ready answer in the traditional ways we have understood to ask the
question. The verses from Psalm 103, in contrast to more truculent
verses the Psalter has to offer, impart a presence, a comfort, a bene-
faction, a less clamorous texture, and those are good reasons to rely
upon them and similar lines from the psalms. In a pleasant way, the
contiguity lines of Psalm 103 of comfort, patience, and affirmation
can be agreeably reminiscent of certain poems we've come to know
by many other poets that do not growl, yell, intimidate, or combat,
but restore through their mere presence and then linger in unhur-
ried generosity.

• • •

When W. H. Auden penned to me the message, "I don't believe
there is such an animal as Twentieth Century Man," I initially
thought of it as a throwaway line in the context of the letter he
had written. Later I realized, upon re-reading and giving his comments further thought and amplification, that the words had, in
fact, summarized emphatically both his literary and theological views about a critical issue: the original psalmists, Coverdale,
Auden, and the committee all shared a commonality that could
not meaningfully be disrupted, for the words of the psalmists and
their thoughts, pains, and humanity conveyed the aspirations,
personal disappointments, happiness and unhappiness of Coverdale and Auden, and all of us who happen to be walking around
at various points along the continuum of time. We are somehow
the same, regardless of the moment in which we find ourselves
alive, which may range from the hell of the Holocaust to convivial
peace passing our way from hour to hour. Through the seeming
simulacrum of a cute throwaway line, Auden had, however, once

again returned to the towering conundrum of time and eternity for which he and Charles Williams had sought to find an answer in the Eucharist, where Auden found the dead and the unborn linked, and in Latin, where he and Williams found a language of the dead but also of the faithful, and where Auden chose to plumb the depths of the immutable, unchallenged question of time and eternity in his Christmas Oratorio, "For the Time Being." In an ironic way, the final product of the committee fulfilled the proposition Auden broached: we took the words of poems written some 2,500–3,000 years ago, collected them, unchanged in personality or character, dressed them in a modern and postmodern garb, and had them sing in the lilts and sonorities we inherited from the sixteenth century of Miles Coverdale, traversing and coalescing a sort of timelessness where Auden meets the poets of the psalms, and all voices convene in a timeless engagement. Whether he knew it or not, the Episcopal Psalter did become, in its final form and edification, a sort of unambiguous and tailored homage to Auden's credo that "I don't think there is such an animal as Twentieth Century Man."

It was Charles Guilbert through whom I found my way into the world and words of the Episcopal psalms, and it was W. H. Auden and those many other poets through whom I found my way to the plentitude, the simple, but conspicuous and unrelenting moment of words in the first place. So it would be to poets I must return in certitude and gratitude for the primal lust that one may call curiosity and another call faithfulness to pursue at the time, as part of all time, the path Miles Coverdale uncovered—a path that would lead us to those very first psalmist voices in a completely separate land of nearly primordial jaggedness to praise and beacon what and whom they did not know, but what and whom they came to know, possibly much better than we. And to them we did return.

APPENDIX I

◠◡

Additional Examples of Literary Devices Employed by Thomas Cranmer in the Book of Common Prayer (1549/1552)

Alliteration: With words of close proximity, repetition of initial consonant sounds.

> The Ordre for the Buriall of the Dead (1549):
>
> . . . besechyng thyne infinite goodnesse, to geve us grace . . .

Assonance: With words of close proximity, repetition of initial vowel sounds.

> An Ordre for Mattyns dayly through the yere (1549); Benedicite omnia opera domini domino:
>
> O ye seas, and floudes, speake good of the Lord . . .

Asyndeton: Absence of conjunctions in an abbreviated series between words, clauses, or phrases.

> The Supper of the Lorde, and the holy Communion, commonly called the Masse (1549):
>
> We praise thee, we blesse thee, we worship thee, we glorifie thee, wee geve thankes to thee for thy greate glory . . .

Chiasmus: Inversion of syntactic elements for parallel clauses or phrases.

> The Supper of the Lorde, and the holy Communion, commonly called the Masse (1549):
>
> . . . wee bee made one with Christ, and Christ with us . . .

(The words "bee made one" are assumed to be part of "Christ bee made one with us" for the second parallel clause; over time, this parallel structure was often simply shortened by many to become: "We in Him, and He in us.")

Epimone: A phrase, question, or clause repeated in a series of connected thoughts or concepts.

An Ordre for Mattyns dayly through the yere (1549); Benedicite omnia opera domini domino:

O ALL ye workes of the Lorde, speake good of the Lorde; prayse hym, and set hym up for ever.

O ye Angels of the Lorde, speake good of the Lorde; prayse hym, and set hym up for ever.

O ye heavens, speake good of the Lorde; prayse hym, and set him up for ever.

Parallelism: A clause or set of words within individual lines having a similar structure and related concepts to other immediately proximate lines.

An Ordre for Mattyns dayly through the yere (1549); Te Deum Laudamus:

The gloryous company of the Apostles, praise thee.
The goodly felowshyp of the Prophetes, praise thee.
The noble armie of Martyrs, praise thee.

Parataxis: A series of clauses, often containing complements of a complete sentence, linked by normal conjunctions, such as "and," "but," "or," etc.

Of The Administracion of publyke Baptisme (1549):

Almyghtie and everlastyng God, whiche of thy justice dydest destroy by fluddes of water the whole worlde for synne, excepte persones, whome of thy mercy (the same tyme) thou didest save in the Arke: <u>And</u> when thou didest drowne in the read sea wycked kyng Pharao with al his armie, yet (at the same time) thou didest leade thy people the chyldren of Israel safely through the myddes therof: wherby thou didest fygure the washyng of thy holy Baptisme: <u>and</u> by the Baptisme of thy wel beloved sonne Jesus Christe, thou dydest sanctifie the fludde Jordan, and al other waters to this misticall washing away of synne: We beseche thee (for thy infinite mercies) that thou wilt mercifully looke upon these children, and sanctifie them with thy holy gost, that by this holesome laver of regeneracion, whatsoever synne is in them, may be washed cleane away, that they being delivered from thy wrathe, may be received into the arke of Christes churche, and so saved from peryshyng: <u>and</u> beeyng fervente in spirite, stedfaste in fayth, joyfull through hope, rooted in charitie, maye ever serve thee: And finally attayne to everlasting lyfe, with all thy holy and chosen people.

༄

Additional Examples of Literary Devices Employed by Miles Coverdale in the Psalms of the Great Bible of 1540

Alliteration: With words of close proximity, repetition of initial consonant sounds.

> . . . for he flourisheth as a flower of the field. (Psalm 103:15b)

Anaphora: Initial words for one clause or phrase repeated at the beginning of successive clauses or phrases.

> The floods are risen, O Lord, the floods have lifted up their noise, the floods lift up their waves. (Psalm 93:4)

Anthimeria: Use of a noun for a verb or similar replacement of normal word usage.

> For I knowledge my faults . . . (Psalm 51:3)

Assonance: With words of close proximity, repetition of initial vowel sounds.

> . . . but yet the Lord that dwelleth on high is mightier. (Psalm 93:5b)

Asyndeton: Absence of conjunctions in an abbreviated series between words, clauses, or phrases.

> Thou rulest the raging of the sea, thou stillest the waves thereof when they arise.
> Thou hast subdued Egypt and destroyed it, thou hast scattered thine enemies abroad with thy mighty arm. (Psalm 89:10–11)

Chiasmus: Inversion of syntactic elements for parallel clauses or phrases.

> I have found David my servant; with my holy oil have I anointed him.
>   (Psalm 89:21)

Epimone: A phrase, question, or clause repeated in a series of connected thoughts or concepts.

> O give thanks unto the Lord, for he is gracious; and his mercy
>   endureth for ever.
> O give thanks unto the God of all gods, for his mercy endureth
>   for ever.
> O thank the Lord of all lords, for his mercy endureth for ever . . .
>   (Psalm 136:1–3)

Hyperbaton: Emphasis of a clause by adjusting the normal order of the words.

> Sing we merrily unto God our strength . . . (Psalm 81:1)

Parataxis: A series of clauses, often containing complements of a complete sentence, linked by normal conjunctions, such as "and," "but," "or," etc.

> But his delight is in the law of the Lord; <u>and</u> in his law will he
>   exercise himself day and night.
> <u>And</u> he shall be like a tree planted by the waterside that will
>   bring forth his fruit in due season. (Psalm 1:2–3)

Simile: A comparison between two unlike objects or concepts using "as" or "like" for relating them.

> For my days are consumed away like smoke, and my bones
>   are burnt up as it were a firebrand. (Psalm 102:3)

Permissions